*8*STEPS TO STARTING A BUSINESS

How to Quickly Gain the
Skills You'll Need

JOHN B. VINTURELLA, PH.D.

8 STEPS TO STARTING A BUSINESS
HOW TO QUICKLY GAIN THE SKILLS YOU'LL NEED

iUniverse books may be ordered through booksellers or by contacting:

iUniverse
1663 Liberty Drive
Bloomington, IN 47403
www.iuniverse.com
1-800-Authors (1-800-288-4677)

Because of the dynamic nature of the Internet, any web addresses or links contained in this book may have changed since publication and may no longer be valid. The views expressed in this work are solely those of the author and do not necessarily reflect the views of the publisher, and the publisher hereby disclaims any responsibility for them.

Any people depicted in stock imagery provided by Thinkstock are models, and such images are being used for illustrative purposes only. Certain stock imagery © Thinkstock.

ISBN: 978-1-5320-2152-7 (sc)
ISBN: 978-1-5320-2153-4 (e)

Library of Congress Control Number: 2017908702

Print information available on the last page.

iUniverse rev. date: 06/24/2017

TABLE OF CONTENTS

PREFACE

Can entrepreneurship be taught? In the broadest sense of the term, the answer is probably no. But many of the skills of successful entrepreneurs can be taught, and sensitivity to business opportunity can be sharpened. A thorough and orderly approach to business planning allows us to assess whether an opportunity exists, and to chart the best way to take maximum advantage of that opportunity. From there, a hardy individual can decide, with a little less uncertainty, whether or not to pursue that opportunity.

After teaching a course in entrepreneurship several times to college seniors and MBA students, at two different universities, using several different textbooks, I detected a need for a new kind of self-study and classroom book. This, therefore, is a highly interactive text that departs somewhat, in content and technique, from traditional approaches.

The concepts of entrepreneurship cannot be absorbed passively; they are based on powers of observation and critical thinking, development of skills in estimating and projecting economic results, and the integration and application of knowledge from coursework, life experience, and attempts at understanding human nature.

First of all, this text contains a lot more questions than answers, because for most of the issues we consider there is no one right answer. Some of the questions asked have an apparent response, many have several responses which are equally appropriate, and a few are purely rhetorical. What is most important is that the questions be provocative, causing the reader to think, to search for applicable experience, and to find that answer that is "right" for the reader.

Case studies are integral to achieving our objectives. After some market research we discuss (often through minicases) the concepts applicable to some stage of the entrepreneurial process; the full cases then "drive home" these concepts by demonstrating them in action. One of these case studies threads its way through the entire text, describing the consequences of decisions made at various stages of a business on its later fortunes over a period of 20 years; not coincidentally, I was intimately involved in those decisions. I hope these cases help your entrepreneurial development as much as they have mine.

Another feature of the text is that it is centered on the business plan. After some basic concepts are treated, and an opportunity is selected, its evaluation and refinement are treated in the context of the appropriate section of the business plan. It has been my experience that this approach gives a structure to the planning process that makes it less intimidating, and more effective.

While this basically designed as a self-study course, we do have supplementary materials for a teacher who would like to use this as a text. Contact me (jbv@jbv.com) to discuss which of these materials are available.

To the self-studier:

The objective of this text is summarized by the subtitle, *"How to Quickly Gain the Skills You'll Need."* With these skills we expect that you will find that starting a business doesn't have to be complicated. We treat the entrepreneurial process as a series of eight steps, each step clearly defined and capable of being mastered.

To get the most from the book do the homework, answer the review questions, and extract all you can from the case studies. Build a business plan for your proposed venture while applying the lessons learned through this program.

The Internet will almost certainly be your primary source of information, but you may wish to follow stories in the newspaper and periodicals where the subject bears on what you are studying here. These might be about business incubators, funding of ventures, and success stories. These will keep you current in the field and will often add depth to your understanding.

Note to students using this as a textbook:

Few challenges that I face in the course of operating my business are as daunting as facing a class in Entrepreneurship. Students are not always receptive to the most applied and least structured course of their college careers.

My primary objective is to create an atmosphere that is more like business than school, where the premium is on initiative and independent thinking rather than retention of facts, and where the student's opinions and judgment are respected and sharpened. To achieve this, I try to function more as a facilitator or group leader than a teacher.

To get the most from this approach, you must immerse yourself in the class dynamic, joining the management analysis and decision-making team. Read the text, prepare the cases, "ponder" the discussion questions, and turn in brief answers to case questions at the start of class. Active participation in the class discussion then expands on and supplements the readings and cases.

Show some original thinking and critical reading, bring in examples of our discussion topics from the business and popular literature, and collect particularly meaningful or inspiring quotations. Most of all, get involved, and enjoy!

"Entrepreneurship"

is a derivative of the French word "entreprendre,"
which means "to undertake,
to pursue opportunities, to fulfill needs
and wants through innovation."

"Tell me and I'll forget; show me and I may remember;
involve me and I'll understand."

Chinese Proverb

STEP 1

Think like an Entrepreneur

Chapter Objectives:

On completing this chapter, you should be able to:

- Define entrepreneurship, and discuss the characteristics of an entrepreneur
- Compare your personal characteristics and preferences to a profile of widely recognized characteristics of successful entrepreneurs
- Examine your attitude toward risk within the context of the requirements of a startup venture
- Evaluate business ideas as opportunities
- Generate business ideas from your knowledge and interests
- Understand how people are motivated to "take the plunge."

a. What Is Entrepreneurship?

(1) Introduction

Entrepreneurship is the process of creating or seizing an opportunity, and pursuing it regardless of the resources currently controlled. The American Heritage Dictionary defines an entrepreneur to be "a person who organizes, operates, and assumes the risk for business ventures."

These are rather abstract concepts for a person just beginning to consider whether they ought to start a business rather than take a job, or leave a secure job for a chance at greater self-fulfillment. Let us try to refine our understanding of entrepreneurship by asking some more specific questions.

Is everyone who runs a business an entrepreneur? What about the newspaper carrier, shoeshine person, grass cutter? Does it matter whether these are full or part-time pursuits? At what scope does self-employment as a choice become a "venture?" Is a "lifestyle" business, with no plan for growth, an entrepreneurial venture? Does it matter what we call it?

Entrepreneurship is more an attitude than a skill or a profession. We may each answer these questions differently, yet all answer appropriately within our own frame of reference.

Would you consider a person who inherits a business an entrepreneur? It is their own money and financial security at risk. They could as easily liquidate, invest in blue-chips, and live off dividends.

Would living off your success as a stock-picker be an entrepreneurial venture? What if you did it in addition to holding a full-time job?

Would a person who inherited a small or marginal business, then took it to new dimensions be considered an entrepreneur? What if that person paced the business' decline to just carry them to retirement? Is long-term success, even beyond the founder's lifetime, an important criterion to being an entrepreneur?

Are franchise owners entrepreneurs? Franchises are sure things, aren't they? Is it much different from income from "passive" investments? What is the appeal of franchise ownership?

Are there entrepreneurs in large companies? How can a company promote "intrapreneurship?" Are different qualities required of a successful division manager than of a president of a successful company of similar size? Is an entrepreneur necessarily a manager?

Entrepreneurship is generally characterized by some type of innovation, a significant investment, and a strategy that values expansion. The manager is generally charged with using existing resources to make a business run well. Are these incompatible roles? Are most managers entrepreneurial?

These questions have no one "correct" answer, but are meant to stimulate your assessing your view of entrepreneurship. This is often a useful first step in deciding whether some entrepreneurial pursuit might become a part of your career path.

(2) Self-Analysis

Peter F. Drucker, author of *Innovation and Entrepreneurship*, said that anybody from any organization can learn how to be an entrepreneur, that it is "systematic work." But there is a difference between learning how to be, and succeeding as an entrepreneur.

"When a person earns a degree in physics, he becomes a physicist," said Morton Kamien, a former professor of entrepreneurship at Northwestern University. "But if you were to earn a degree in entrepreneurship, that wouldn't make you an entrepreneur."

What does make a person a likely "candidate" to be a successful entrepreneur? Several "yardsticks" have been proposed, but the real challenge is in accurately applying them to ourselves.

The U.S. Small Business Administration suggests that we begin by examining our motivation. How important to you are the reasons commonly given for people going into business for themselves? Among these reasons are freedom from work routine; being your own boss; doing what you want when you want; boredom with the current job; financial desires, and; a perceived opportunity. Which of these might be sufficient to get you to take the risk?

Personal characteristics required, according to the SBA (https://www.sba.gov/starting-business/how-start-business/entrepreneurship-you), include leadership, decisiveness, and competitiveness. Can you objectively rate yourself in these dimensions? How much of each of these traits is enough to insure a good chance of success? Important factors in personal style include will-power, and self-discipline, comfort with the planning process, and with working with others. Are these indicators of success even for the non-entrepreneurial?

The prospective entrepreneur should perform a personal skills inventory that includes supervisory/managerial experience, business education, knowledge about the specific business of interest, and willingness to acquire any necessary skills that may be missing. A commitment to filling any knowledge or experience gap is a very positive indicator of success.

Former newspaper columnist Niki Scott suggested questions that could help us determine our fitness for the temperamental demands of entrepreneurship:

Do you routinely accept responsibility? Are you comfortable with moderate risk?

Do you consider yourself pro-active? Focused? A priority-setter?

Are you confident about overcoming obstacles? Realistic about your limitations?

Are you accurate? Controlled? Self-reliant? Disciplined? A self-starter?

Are you comfortable accepting advice? Willing to do whatever it takes?

Are you fair and honest? Constructive? A good delegator? A motivator?

Are you persevering? Resilient? Do you know when to quit?

Does it still sound like fun? How does the sense of intensity and personal responsibility implied by this checklist sit with you? Does this direction still seem a few years away?

(3) Opportunity Mindset

The process of creating or seizing an opportunity is less the result of a deliberate search than it is a mindset of maintaining a form of vigilance that is sensitized to business opportunity. This frequently relates to the prospective entrepreneur's current profession or interests, where he or she perceives a process that can be more efficiently performed an attractive new service or improvement of an existing service, or some business or geographic "niche" that is being underserved.

Successful entrepreneurs exhibit the ability to recognize an opportunity while it is still taking shape. These are often based on broad trends, which may be: demographic, such as the "graying" of America, creating opportunities in health services; sociological developments, like the "green" movement, with its emphasis on recycling and environmental sensitivity, and; cultural changes caused by changing economic conditions and technological developments.

Opportunities can also frequently be found in current and developing business trends such as the globalization of business, the need for outsourcing created by downsizing, and the burgeoning service economy. There are often localized opportunities, based on geography, natural resources, human resources in local abundance, and the like. Can you think of any for your area?

Resource: Springwise (https://www.springwise.com/) – With a network of observers around the globe, Springwise "looks for the most promising business ventures, ideas and concepts that are ready for regional or international adaptation, expansion, partnering, investments or cooperation."

(4) The Risk Factor

Why isn't everyone an entrepreneur?

Obviously, no opportunity is a sure thing, even though the path to riches has been described as, simply "...you make some stuff, sell it for more than it cost you... that's all there is except for a few million details." The devil is in those details, and if one is not prepared to accept the possibility of failure, one should not attempt a business start-up.

It is not indicative of a negative perspective to say that an analysis of the possible reasons for failure enhances our chances of success. Can you say "failure is no big deal?" Can you separate failure of an idea from personal failure? As scary as it is to think about, many of the great entrepreneurial success stories started with a failure or two.

Entire books are devoted to the subject of why small businesses fail, but the reason is generally one, or a combination, of the following: *inadequate financing* often due to overly optimistic sales projections; *management shortcomings*, including inadequate financial controls, lax customer credit, inexperience, and neglect, and; *misreading the market*, often indicated by a failure to reach the "critical mass" required in sales volume and profitability due to competitive disadvantages or general industry weakness.

Some types of failure can indicate that we may not be entrepreneurial material. Foremost is reaching one's level of incompetence; if I am a great programmer, will I be a great software company president? Attitudinal problems can also be fatal, such as excessive focus on financial rewards, without the willingness to put in the work and attention required. Addressing these possibilities requires an objectivity about ourselves that not everyone can manage.

Other types of failure can be recovered from if you "learned your lesson." The most common explanation for these is that "it seemed like a good idea at the time." More specifically, we may have sought too big a "kill;" we could have looked past the flaws in a business concept because it was a business we wanted to be in. The venture could have been the victim of a muddled business concept, a weak business plan, or (more often) the absence of a plan. Sometimes factors outside our control can play a part, such as a natural disaster or recession, and may offer little information as to our "entrepreneurial mettle."

Are there any safeguards against failure? No! Even the best conceived and implemented business ventures can become market experiments that simply did not work. Our goal here is to apply a process to the planning of entrepreneurial ventures that can greatly minimize risk. That is the best that we can do, and the degree to which we can enhance our confidence about a venture must enter into any decision about its pursuit.

One of the best approaches requires patience, and to a commitment to preparation well in advance of start-up. This could be a long-range process of getting to better understand one's strengths, weaknesses, and limitations, and setting about filling knowledge and experience gaps.

We are all self-employed; even as employees of a firm, we are still primarily personal career managers. The path to an entrepreneurial venture might begin by earning a salary in the business one expects to enter, while learning more about it, and waiting for the opportune time to go out on one's own. This time can be used to develop a support network, professional and personal, and generating ideas to "bounce off" people whose opinion one respects.

Once an idea is thought to represent a real opportunity, one must be able to research the market, know what data is important and how to gather it meaningfully, and know what actions this information indicates. This can then be worked into a rather detailed plan, and then refined into a blueprint for success.

In a *Wall Street Journal* article Ken Elias described "Why My Business Failed." He offers some rather tangible suggestions that could be useful in such a blueprint:

- Don't budget your expectations.
  Nothing happens according to plan; things happen not incrementally but in bundles. Sales and expenses come in lumps; in cash flow, plan for the worst.

- Beware of cheap help.
  Inexperienced or incompetent employees consume your precious time in guidance and damage control. Good employees make good impressions.

- Talk the vision, sell the reality.
  Talk about what you see in the future, but only sell what you can actually deliver.

- Even if the concept is right, it won't fly if the strategy is wrong.
  Acknowledge that it is more likely than not for your strategy to be wrong, and be prepared to change it.

- Appoint a Board of Directors for oversight.
  Your point of view is distorted from being too close to the venture.

- Great meetings don't mean sales.
  Find customers that are ready to buy today.

Elias concluded by asking himself whether he would start another business today:

"Absolutely. The experience is fabulous, exciting and the possibility of success is always there. But next time I'll follow my own advice."

This advice was hard-won. We hope to let the lessons of others ease your path, and will begin with a discussion of recognizing and evaluating opportunities.

b. Small Business Opportunities

(1) Opportunity Defined

"An opportunity is attractive, durable, and timely and is anchored in a product or service that creates or adds value for its buyer or end user. Opportunities are created because there are changing circumstances, inconsistencies, chaos, lags, or leads, information gaps, and a variety of other vacuums, and because there are entrepreneurs who can recognize and seize them." (Source: Jeff Timmons, *New Venture Creation*)

What businesses are currently in rapid change and uncertainty? Where is today's chaos? Where are our area's lags, leads, and gaps? Do we see a service vacuum we could help fill?

Ideas may be easy enough to generate, but an idea is not necessarily an opportunity! Building a "better mousetrap" does not insure success; other factors include fit, timing, and resources.

For an idea to be an opportunity:

- The "window of opportunity" is opening, and will remain open long enough.
  My section of town is growing rapidly, and services are not quite keeping up. "People" are saying that we desperately need a good coffee shop, and an office supply store. We cannot be the only entrepreneurs that perceive this. How long before the need becomes compelling enough for others to jump in? (Who are these people? Are they just in our immediate circle? Are they representative enough of the area from which to extrapolate?)

- Entry is feasible, and achievable with the committed principals.
  Two friends want to be partners with me in a venture; one is managing a coffee shop across town, and willing to manage a startup. We could muster the capital for a coffee shop, but an office supply store seems outside our reach.

- The proposed venture has some competitive advantage. We were among the first to locate in the new area, and are very active in the local business community. We know of an ideal site, and the building manager is a friend. She is willing to sub-contract the beverage and light-meal/dessert services the building provides tenants.

- The economics of the venture are "rewarding and forgiving."
  Materials costs are a small percentage of revenues; site preparation and equipment costs are minimal.

We can break even at what seems to be an easily achievable volume.

Being first to the market with a good idea does not insure success unless one can preempt competition by quickly grabbing a large market share, or by erecting other barriers to the entry of competitors. Could we withstand Starbucks' entry into the market?

(2) Systematic Search for Opportunities

Where do business ideas come from? The best place to start is with what you know. Most often, they come from work experience and personal interests, such as hobbies; other sources of ideas can be friends and relatives, and our educational background.

The idea generating process can be "seeded" by market research. For example, *Forbes Magazine* suggests 11 industries for "hot" startups: https://www.forbes.com/pictures/efgg45kmfg/11-industries-for-hot-start-ups/#56a763996c0b. *Entrepreneur Magazine* has information on how to conduct market research for your business idea: https://www.entrepreneur.com/article/70518.

Many services are highly localized. Is national data useful to your consideration of a neighborhood coffee shop? What about data for the metropolitan area of which you want to serve the northeast corner, and 18% of the population? Can we acquire meaningful data on just our market area? Is current data as useful as future projections?

For an indication of where we might best expend our efforts, let's take a look at where the jobs are now. This gives an idea of the relative magnitude of the various sectors of the economy (see Figure 1-1).

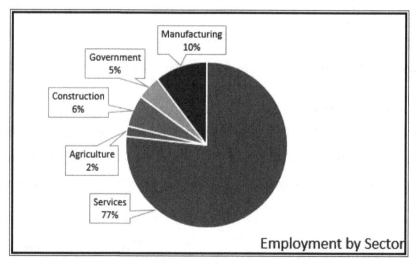

Figure 1-1

Why do service businesses seem to dominate job growth? Is it that people today value time and convenience, which services produce, over more tangible products? Is automation providing productivity gains that are allowing increasing demand to be satisfied with relatively few additional workers? Or is it that services must be produced locally, whereas goods for local consumption can be produced anywhere in the world?

Certainly, service industry growth is good news for prospective entrepreneurs. Service businesses are relatively easy to start, and economies of scale are not generally sufficient to give larger companies a significant competitive edge.

Is there a down side to job growth being dominated by the service industry? Will we become a nation of "burger-flippers?" Can "brain-power" be a service? What forms might this take? Can it be exported? Is there some consulting function you can perform that people need? What skills do you have that separate you from "the masses?" Can this be turned into a business?

With which service businesses do you enjoy doing business? What distinguishes their service from other similar businesses? What lessons can you draw for any business you might start? It is not enough anymore to just say that you put the customer first; there must be meaningful, tangible evidence.

(3) "Brainstorming" and Trend-Tracking

Demographic and cultural changes are creating opportunities. Futurist Faith Popcorn, in *The Popcorn Report*, suggests some broad areas of cultural and psychographic change that are creating

new areas of opportunity (https://lbbonline.com/news/
the-5-trends-marketers-cant-afford-to-ignore-in-2017/):

1. IRL (In Real Life) / Micro-Clanning

Wary of being phished, cat-fished or otherwise hoodwinked
online, people will meet to connect and share in-person.
Intimacy will fight out digital isolation. It's an opportunity for
marketers to create better experiences for consumers, IRL.

2. AI will probably take our jobs.

But there's an upside to more free time. Brands can use AI to
make people's lives more enjoyable when they're working less.

3. Data (Gold) Mining

The next generation of consumers, Gen Z, is privacy obsessed.
Brands must get ready to pay for their precious data.

4. EMOnomics

Emotion is the new currency – from joy to misery. As
our culture becomes more divisive, we want our moods
expressed and recognized. Brands can cash in if they appeal
to consumers' emotional selves.

5. Small-ing

Big is no longer trustworthy. Consumers are shrinking their
networks. Brands need to make themselves seem smaller to
earn consumers' trust.

Popcorn suggests that a venture that "taps into" two or more of these needs in a competitive way will be a winner. Which of these does your idea address?

More specific ideas are often suggested in the business and entrepreneurship literature. *Inc. Magazine* suggests that the following are the best industries for startups (http://www. inc.com/ss/best-industries-for-starting-a-business)

Meditation and mindfulness training

Increased corporate spending on programs to improve employee focus has helped boost an industry that research firm IBISWorld values at $1.1 billion in the U.S. App-based training is bringing the practice to an even broader audience.

Ready-to-drink coffee and tea

Consumers are ditching mixes and concentrates in favor of on-the-go coffee and tea, largely driven by health innovations. From 2013 to 2015, U.S. sales of these drinks nearly tripled, landing at $143 million, according to the nonprofit Specialty Food Association.

Mobility tech

This industry offers startups potential partnerships with and acquisition by large tech companies and automakers working on autonomous vehicles. Ford, for example, invested

$1 billion in Pittsburgh-based Argo AI in its effort to develop a self-driving car by 2021.

Pet care

Tech innovations are making over this industry, which is valued at $60 billion in the U.S. Revenue for pet grooming and boarding alone was nearly $8 billion in the U.S. in 2016, according to IBISWorld, which projects it to grow 7 percent annually through 2021.

Construction management

Global funding for hardware and software to streamline building projects, or to sell and rent construction equipment, rose to $254 million in 2015 from $51 million in 2010, according to researcher CB Insights--and analysts say it's still an emerging industry.

Synthetic biology

Health and environmental concerns have driven interest in genetically engineered medicines, foods, and fuel. It's a costly and technical field, but payoffs can be huge for companies like DNA manufacturing company Twist Bioscience.

Computer vision

Advancements in artificial intelligence have produced companies working to interpret and act on visual data. The technology, which attracted $522 million and 69 deals in

2016, can be applied to child development, social media networks, and web analytics.

Brick-and-mortar retail technology

Startups are helping modernize in-store operations. One notable example is London-based Iconeme, which created technology that pushes product information from mannequins to nearby shoppers' smartphones.

Do you see an opportunity in one of these areas?

Are these types of opportunity listings useful? Is it already too late by the time a type of business is publicly acknowledged to be an opportunity? Is it better to wait for the "first movers" to clarify exactly what services consumers want, and then enter with a more focused product?

The best source for current information is, of course, the Internet. Check the web sites of the leading companies in the field you wish to enter. Find the major issues for the industry and consider how you might address them. Get statistics on the size of the industry, and in what direction sales are going. Assess the chances for a new venture in this field.

Keep up with the major periodicals, including the business section of your local newspaper. Broad trends can be tracked by being a reasonably well-informed observer of the popular culture.

Exercise 1: **Opportunity Scan**

Do a search on opportunities that fit your strengths and interests.

Describe a specific business that would take advantage of one of these opportunities.

What are your strengths and weaknesses for developing such a venture?

What are the critical factors to success of the venture?

Do we need to move into a "hot" new business, or are better approaches to well-established industries just as promising? Do you think more people have gotten rich with new computer software products, or with McDonald's franchises? Is there a family business that you can take to a new location, or otherwise higher levels?

Once we are comfortable that we have a sense of where the opportunities are, and which of those we might be equipped to take advantage of, we are ready to advance into a more purposeful set of steps that we will call the entrepreneurial process.

c. The Entrepreneurial Process

While the conditions under which people start or acquire businesses vary greatly, certain steps may be considered common to all:

(1) Commitment

Do I really want to start or own a business? Am I willing to take on the personal demands of entrepreneurship? Can I live without a regular paycheck, a predictable work schedule, and for a while without vacations and other benefits?

Is there a product or service that fits my talents or desires? Am I ready yet? Can I muster the resources to make the venture a success? Am I prepared for the possibility that I might lose my money and property, and do damage to my health and self-respect?

For women and minorities, there are additional considerations relevant to their chances of success. Why is it more difficult for them? How much is due to discrimination and skepticism by the support structure, and how much is due to a "confidence gap" within the principals? Do they have to be "better" to make it, or is entrepreneurship the only true meritocracy? Is any disadvantage only at startup?

(2) Selection

The basic rule is simple: "Find a market need and fill it!" The process of finding the need, and the method chosen to fill it are where the difficulties arise.

Based on my opportunity scan, does the market need a product or service that is not currently being provided? Is there a needed product or service currently being provided in a less than satisfactory way? Is some particular market being underserved due to capacity shortages or location gaps? Can I serve any of these needs with some competitive advantage?

What type of business could best seize this opportunity? Do I need partners? Where will I locate? Whom would we serve, and how? Would my chances be improved by buying a franchise or an existing business, as opposed to starting a venture "from scratch?" How do I go about evaluating the possibilities? How much study is warranted? What type of information is relevant?

(3) Planning

Once a business idea is selected, the concept must be sharpened by a detailed planning process. The result of this step is a comprehensive business plan, with its major components being the marketing "mix", the strategic plan, operational and logistical structures, and the financial proposal.

Marketing mix issues focus on how the product or service is differentiated from the competition. A business can differentiate itself on any of what are often referred to as the "four P's" of marketing: product characteristics, price structure, place or method of distribution, and/or promotional strategy. How did our neighborhood coffee shop differentiate itself?

Strategic issues relate broadly to the company's mission and goals. Every venture must continually assess its strengths and weaknesses, the opportunities to be seized, and any threats to the success and future plans of the business.

Operational issues relate to company structure, and to the more tangible items such as location, equipment, and methods of distribution. Decisions on these issues largely determine startup costs.

The financial proposal includes an estimate of the amount of money needed to start the venture, to absorb losses during the start-up period, and to provide sufficient working capital to avoid cash shortages. It projects sales and profitability over some period into the future, generally 3 to 5 years. Where outside funding is sought, it also describes distribution of ownership of the venture and methods of debt repayment and/or buyback of partial ownership

(4) Implementation

The business plan is the "blueprint" for the implementation process. It focuses on the four major sub-plans: marketing; strategy; operational/logistic, and; financial. Actions to be performed that are not specifically described in the plan involve finding lenders or investors, identifying a business or franchise to buy where appropriate, determining a specific business location, and conducting the negotiations and acquiring the permits required to get to a "customer-ready" condition.

We will now assume that the reader is past the commitment step, and concentrate on the latter three steps in the entrepreneurial process in the next two chapters. Before doing that, however, we will build some added perspective on the nature of small business.

d. The Nature of Small Business

Forbes Magazine has compiled several statistics that give us a sense of the importance of small business to the American economy (https://www.forbes.com/sites/jasonnazar/2013/09/09/16-surprising-statistics-about-small-businesses/#28d688695ec8). The following are among the more significant:

1. The SBA defines a small business as an enterprise having **fewer than 500 employees**
2. There are almost **28 million small businesses** in the US and over 22 million are self-employed with no additional payroll or employees (these are called nonemployers)
3. **Over 50%** of the working population (120 million individuals) **works in a small business**
4. Small businesses have generated over **65% of the net new jobs** since 1995
5. Approximately **543,000 new businesses** get started **each month** (but more employer businesses shut down than start up each month)
6. 7 out of 10 new employer **firms survive** at least 2 years, **half at least 5 years**, a third at least 10 years and a quarter stay in business 15 years or more
7. **52%** of all small businesses are **home-based**

What does small business have to do with entrepreneurship? A small business is the usual product of entrepreneurship. SBA reports that more than a third of business start-ups consist of one employee (see Figure 1-2). What kinds of businesses can you enter with only one employee? Can a person start a large business?

Only 3% of businesses employ over 25 people at start-up. What kinds of businesses are the larger start-ups likely to be?

The number of small businesses in the United States is on the order of 30 million. Small businesses (defined as businesses with fewer than 500 employees) account for 99.7% of all businesses in the US.

Small businesses are characterized by independent management, closely-held ownership, a primarily local area of operations, and a scale that is small in comparison with competitors. They can be "lifestyle" businesses, where the primary objective is employment for the principals, or "entrepreneurial ventures," with a commitment to substantial growth in scale of operations and profitability.

Why do people start small businesses? The reasons are varied, but cluster around five basic objectives. The primary motivation for most business start-ups is to allow the entrepreneur to achieve independence; money is secondary. Is this surprising? What is your motivation?

The other reasons named most often are that an opportunity presented itself, a person took over the family business, or that the person simply wanted to be an entrepreneur. For context, what is the appeal of corporate life? Of a government job? A union job? Rich parents?

What kind of people start their own businesses? Are skills any different from working in a large business? Do they need to be their own boss because they are social misfits, or otherwise incapable of working for other people? The opposite is more often the case.

Most entrepreneurs have similar personal characteristics, including the desire to control their own destiny. This confidence leads to their valuing control, freedom, flexibility; and self-reliance. They generally value achievement over money, contrary to the popular notion. They desire responsibility and personal fulfillment.

Most entrepreneurs are not "gamblers;" they have a preference for moderate risk (How moderate do you think?). They are always searching for opportunities, and willing to pursue some.

More successful entrepreneurs tend to be proactive, assertive, and highly observant. They are efficient, quality-conscious, and good at planning and procedures. As business operators, they are committed to "partnership" with employees, customers, suppliers, and their community. Would these skills or personality traits lead to success at any venture? Which are vital for success as corporate employees? Are start-ups for overachievers only? What are the chances for any person willing to work hard, set goals, and be accountable for the results?

Some of the more tangible characteristics of new businesses and their owners were measured in a survey of almost 3,000 businesses commissioned by the National Federation of Small Business and American Express. Among the more interesting findings were that about 64% were startups, and 30% were purchased, with the remainder inherited, promoted or otherwise brought into ownership. About 11% of the businesses operate under a franchise name. Are entrepreneurs born (demanding parents, ethnic tradition) or made? Is it for you? At what age? What else do you need to do to be ready? Can entrepreneurship be taught?

A primary inhibitor of business start-up is that few people have the financial cushion to give up a job for the uncertain income of a start-up venture. In an AT&T/AICPA survey respondents identified inadequate funding as their biggest hurdle (named by 31%). Overall, 28% said lenders were too conservative, 16% reported being unable to find investors, and 12% claimed a lack of collateral.

Even where the start-up investment consists largely of other people's money, the amount of financial risk for the entrepreneur is beyond what most can responsibly handle. For many with the financial means, the stress of bearing complete responsibility for the company's direction and performance is the discouraging factor.

Various estimates have been made for the failure rate of business start-ups, based on various concepts of failure and of appropriate survey methods. There seems to be a consensus that less than half of new businesses survive the start-up "trauma." Perhaps, a major reason for what seems to be a high failure rate is that it is so easy to start a business. There is no institutionalized check of qualifications in the U.S.; on the contrary, our tax dollars fund the Small Business Administration and a number of other agencies and programs to encourage business formation.

The winners tend to be those who can find some competitive edge, even when their product or service is similar to those around them. Marketing professionals often call this edge the "unique selling proposition," or USP. Pinpointing and refining one's USP is not a simple matter. One approach was suggested by Charlotte Taylor in *Entrepreneur Magazine:*

- Put yourself in your customer's shoes; satisfy his or her needs, not yours.
- Know what motivates behavior and buying decisions.
- Find the real reasons people buy your product instead of a competitor's. Ask them!
- "Shop" the competition, be open-minded about your product, and never stop looking for ways to make your product stand out.

Conveying one's USP can be a serious challenge. An approach is unique only in the context of our competitors' marketing messages. We must identify what they say they sell, not just product and service characteristics. For example, Charles Revson, founder of Revlon, insisted that he sold hope, not makeup. Similarly, United Airlines sells "friendly skies," and Wal-Mart sells "always" the low price. Do these slogans convey how each company views their customers? Does their selling proposition appeal to your preferences?

Surveys consistently show the American regard for entrepreneurs; approval of a son or daughter starting a business exceeds 80%. Business owners scored first in a Princeton survey of positive influence of selected groups on "the way things are going," ahead of technology, the church, and environmentalists.

Entrepreneurship is part of our culture, recognized as far back as 1840, when Alexis de Tocqueville, in *Democracy in America*, said "What most astonished me in the United States is not so much the marvelous grandeur of some undertakings as the innumerable multitude of small ones."

Exercise 2: **Company Prospectus**

Recast your business idea in terms of its competitive advantage.

Prepare an industry analysis (size, customers, trends, and competitiveness)

Identify your specific market, and estimate the share you think you can capture.

Summary

While most of us have a fairly clear image of what entrepreneurship is, development of a useful working definition of an entrepreneur is a challenge. This is more than an exercise in semantics; for each of us, our concept of the profile of an entrepreneur can be the basis for evaluating our fitness for the role, deciding whether or not to pursue an entrepreneurial venture, and the timing and scope of that pursuit.

Unlike most other career paths, there is little consensus on how to prepare a person for life as an entrepreneur. Many feel that entrepreneurs are born that way, and that there is no appropriate formal preparation. We contend that, given certain personal characteristics, a person with entrepreneurial interest can be taught an approach to recognizing and evaluating opportunities that will minimize the risk that forms the downside of the business venture.

The necessary personal characteristics are fairly easy to identify. The problem is in objectively evaluating ourselves against measures as subjective as leadership, decisiveness, and competitiveness. Planning and teamworking skills can be developed, but the same can not necessarily be said for will power and self-discipline. Sensitivity to the existence of an opportunity can be sharpened, but our tolerance for risk can be hard to raise.

We can begin our "fearless" self-assessment by seriously considering the following questions:

What are my real reasons for considering going into business? These need to be strong enough to sustain you when the excitement of the startup has passed, and the everyday grind begins.

Do I have an adequate support structure? If you have a spouse, or are relying on some other form of family support, make sure that they understand the sacrifices involved and the pressures these will put on relationships.

Do I respond well to continuous pressure? Startup pressures will suspend vacations and holidays and take up much of your weekends. Even after startup, business concerns seldom end when you lock the door at closing time.

Am I willing to subordinate all other interests and goals, for an indeterminate period, to developing this business? There is more to life than work, and maintaining a balanced and healthy lifestyle can be a challenge for the self-employed.

Fortunately, we do not have to decide right away. There is an entrepreneurial process that we are going to discuss in detail, which takes us through a series of steps that makes the final decision of whether to undertake a venture a fairly clear one. Along the way, we will develop a better understanding of the fit and feel of the actions required to our unique temperament.

The steps in the process may be rather broadly defined as:

1. Commitment: Am I ready to deal with the uncertainty of a regular paycheck, the lack of any structure other than that which I provide?

2. Selection: Is there a market need that I can competitively fill, do I have the necessary information and experience?

3. Planning: What is my strategy, how will I differentiate myself from competitors, what is the sales potential, how quickly can it be achieved?

4. Implementation: Where do I locate, do I need partners, what size and scope of business is called for, how much capital is required?

This chapter has dealt rather broadly with the issue of commitment. The following case study will give us a better sense of the decisions that need to be made after a business idea is selected.

Case Study 1-1	Used-Book Store

INTRODUCTION

"We've got the merchandise and the store; all we need now is an identity."

Dwight Payne summed up the status of a new venture he just initiated with friend Gary Heap. Dwight and Gary reside in Santa Barbara, CA, where they attend college and pursue their mutual hobby of science-fiction book collecting.

"Dwight and I are really into science fiction," Heap explains. "We have pooled our book collection and have over 4,000 volumes - Heinlein, Van Vogt, Asimov, Bester, Moorcock, Pohl. You name the book; it's somewhere in our collection."

"Not only that," Payne adds, "we've got sci-fi magazines going back over twenty-five years. All neatly catalogued and indexed. I'll bet it would cost us $20,000 to assemble this collection today."

Payne and Heap decided that, at the end of this school year, they will dedicate the summer to getting a used-book store started in Santa Barbara as a means of supplementing their income year-round. They elaborate:

Payne: Gary and I figured that we might as well try to capitalize on our love of books and reading. Both of us are familiar with used-book store operations because we have haunted  them so regularly in building our collection. We've been to just about every used-paperback operation in Southern California. A lot of them seem to be profiting.

Heap: My uncle owns a storefront near the University, and we made a deal for him to rebuild it as a used-book store; it's just about finished. He also co-signed an inventory loan for $4,000 for some start-up working capital. In exchange he gets 25 percent of our sales for two years. Not a bad deal, actually, since it is such a good location to serve the hordes of avid readers in town.

Payne: Just three weeks after lining up the building, Gary and I lucked into a deal in Ventura. The owner of a pretty good-sized used-paperback outlet put his merchandise up for sale to raise some quick cash.

Heap: We swung a good deal with him - over 10,000 paperbacks, magazines, and comics for $3,500, and $1,500 for all the shelving we will need. We borrowed the money from some fraternity brothers, rented a U-Haul truck, and carted the stuff home.

Payne: It filled the building about half way. We're currently cataloging the stuff. We got a great deal. Most of the books are in good shape and recent. It's a good mixture of fiction and nonfiction, including westerns, mysteries, gothics, biographies, and a few technical books.

Heap: We're virtually ready to open the doors, but we still haven't decided on what competitive strategy to use. We don't want to be just another used-book store. There are a half-dozen of those around town. We want to be something different in our image and in the way we operate.

Payne: We want to be able to attract customers based on our differentiated image and unique style of operating. We're looking to be something a little different. And profitable!

STUDY QUESTIONS

This case is a "do-it-yourselfer." Rather than passively accepting decisions, policies and estimates, let us generate them ourselves to get a feel for what is involved in roughing out a preliminary plan.

1. The marketing concept

Suggest a marketing concept for the store, including a name.

Who are the customers? What are they looking for?

How will Dwight and Gary meet their needs? (Company image, policies)

How will they get known? (Advertising, promotions, competitive edge)

2. Reality check

Decide on days of the week and hours the store will be open.

Estimate staffing required and hourly salary costs.

Do Dwight and Gary really work for free?

What is a reasonable expectation of customers per day?

Average purchase per customer?

What are pessimistic and optimistic values of these estimates?

How much will they have to spend on advertising and promotion to meet these estimates?

What will they pay, on average, for each book?

How much can they get, on average, for each book?

3. Feasibility Study Worksheet

Estimate the profitability of the venture. Use low, expected, and optimistic sales estimates and estimate a break-even sales level. Make reasonable assumptions where information is missing. Payroll cost may be assumed to be wages paid only. Debt service payments may be assumed to total $400 per month.

Fill in the table on the next page, or use a spreadsheet for the calculations.
Then, answer the burning question:

Would you do it if you were they?

Dwight and Gary's Bookstore   Pro-Forma Income Statement

Monthly Estimates	Low	Expected	Optimistic	Break-even
Sales -				
Cost of Goods =				
Gross Margin				
Payroll +				
Rent +				
Utilities +				
Promotion +				
Debt Svc +				
Other =				
Total Expense				
Profit/Loss				

STEP 2

Consider the Internet

Chapter Objectives:

On completing this chapter, you should be able to:

- Place 20 years of the Internet in a historical perspective
- Relate the Internet to your business idea
- Understand how your website can help to build your business
- Discuss how social media can be a valuable marketing tool
- Evaluate alternate platforms for your business

The Internet has revolutionized entrepreneurship. The following excerpt appeared in the predecessor of this book, written in 1995. I think it is of some historic interest:

Entrepreneurial Resources: The Internet

In the fall of 1994, *Business Week* observed that the Internet "this very public and amorphous collection of computer networks exploded as the techno-fad of the decade." Do not be put off by the word "fad;" the article is titled "The Internet: How it will change the way you do business." There are over 21,000 "storefronts" on the Net, including electronic "malls" and corporate magazines (e.g. IBM's *Think*). The population of the Internet is more than 20 million, and increasing by hundreds of thousands a month worldwide. Median annual income of its citizens is said to be $54,000.

The seers are predicting great things for the Net. David C. Churbuck, in *Forbes*, says that "the day is fast coming when Internet servers and the telephone system will replace the U.S. mail for the delivery of everything from mail-order catalogs to obscure scholarly documents." In *Fortune*, Peter Huber predicts that "Before long the Net will incorporate television and telephone, and all their demographics. The Internet way of delivering information will then swallow up all the others - broadcast, cable, movies, disks..."

Will these promises be realized? Fortunes will be made and lost on attempts to find out. Do you see any possibilities for yourself or your business idea?

For comparison the 1995 Internet population of 20 million has grown to over 3.5 billion worldwide (https://www.statista.com/statistics/273018/number-of-internet-users-worldwide/).

a. Why the Internet?

Why has the Internet become such a powerful business platform? Primarily because startup costs are minimal. Many people start Internet businesses while keeping their day jobs until they feel that sales volume is such that the business can support them.

Once the commitment is made to sell online, the business is now global and open 24/7. If the website is well designed, prospects can be given the impression that you are a major force in the industry.

The Web Doctor (http://www.dbwebdoctor.com/article why companies need a website.asp) says that the Internet "has created a new economy, which by its explosive growth and sheer size already changed our perception of the traditional way of doing business. However, in order to be successful on the net, you don't have to be a giant like them. Many small and mid-size companies managed to build online businesses quite profitably. In fact, studies show small and mid-size companies will be the main growth force of e-commerce in coming years."

Lifehack (http://www.lifehack.org/articles/money/7-reasons-why-you-should-start-your-own-internet-business.html) suggests some of the types of businesses that you can start on the Internet:

- Sell your handmade arts and crafts on Etsy
- Run an informative site that generates revenue through advertisements
- Provide professional services to clients around the world
- Generate client leads for offline businesses
- Sell other peoples' products and earn a commission for each referral

They then proceed to list the reasons why you should start an online business, beginning with job security.

b. Search Engine Optimization

One problem that I have with the Lifehack analysis, and the sales pitch by many Internet service providers, is the assumption that you put up a website and the riches follow. What that leaves out is getting noticed in the marketplace, and that is not easy.

There is an entire industry built on getting you noticed by the search engines. It is called search engine optimization (SEO). The theory is that your SEO consultant knows how Google, for example, rates pages and can structure your web page so as to get you favorable placement.

Search Engine Watch (https://searchenginewatch.com/2016/01/21/seo-basics-22-essentials-you-need-for-optimizing-your-site/) defines SEO as "the umbrella term for all the methods you can use to ensure the visibility of your website and its content on search engine results pages (SERPs)."

Let's say that your webpage currently doesn't show up until page 50 of the search results. Applying SEO to your page you may now show up on page 25. How often do you go to page 25 of search results? Few even go beyond page 1.

To overcome this difficulty, you must be able to anticipate what your prospective customers search for when they are looking for your product or service. What will possibly get you noticed is if you can find one keyword (or key phrase) in this search around which you optimize your page.

Otherwise, there are other ways you can promote your page. Many use social media. If you can afford it, pay-per-click (PPC) advertising may be the way to go.

c. Pay Per Click

Wordstream (http://www.wordstream.com/ppc) describes PPC as "*pay-per-click*, a model of internet marketing in which advertisers pay a fee each time one of their ads is clicked. Essentially, it's a way of buying visits to your site, rather than attempting to "earn" those visits organically."

These ads generally show up at the top of the results page, ahead of what are called "organic" results, which are those based on how high they place with the search engine.

Here are some examples of PPC ads in search engine results:

Try AdWords **Software** Free - WordStream.com
www.wordstream.com/**PPC**-Account-Grader ▾
Use This Simple, Free Tool And Find Your Errors in 60 Seconds. Hurry!
WordStream has 3,014 followers on Google+
Free AdWords Grader - Free PPC Advisor Trial - Subscribe to Newsletter

Warning: Secret **PPC** Tool - Speed**PPC**.com
www.speed**ppc**.com/ ▾
Destroy your **PPC** competition with Proven Patent-pending **Software**.

PPC Management **Software**, **PPC** Bid Management **Software**, Pay ...
www.clicksweeper.com/ ▾
ClickSweeper is **PPC** management **software** for automated keyword bid optimization,
ad management, campaign management and custom reporting.

When an ad is clicked on, the prospective client links to our website. We are charged the PPC amount, and it is then our responsibility to make the sale. We may pay $2 per click for example, and make a $500 sale. These sales must happen often enough to justify the cost of advertising.

d. Social Media

Business News Daily (http://www.businessnewsdaily. com/7832-social-media-for-business.html) has produced a marketer's guide to social media for business. Here is their introduction:

"Social media networks are fantastic resources for businesses of all sizes looking to promote their brands online. The platforms themselves are free to use, and they also have paid advertising options specifically for brands that want to reach even more new audiences. But just because your business should be on social media, that doesn't mean your business should be on every network. It's important that you choose and nurture the social platforms that work best for your business so that you don't spread yourself too thin."

What social networks will work best for you? We will briefly discuss how best to use some of the major networks, but you need to take a deeper look at what audience each reaches and determine the optimal way to use each network in your business. For each of the social media they can be accessed by their name followed by ".com".

(1) Facebook

Facebook is the best-known and biggest social network on the Web. The number of users is said to be more than 1.55 billion active users around the world. Thus your Facebook page makes your business truly global.

For most of its development Facebook was thought of as a social network, but businesses have discovered that it can be used for business purposes. It is generally a supplement to a corporate website and often simply used to capture a potential customer and direct them to the website.

As with all social media, you must find the frequency of postings that works best for your business. Postings might include product information or information on some aspect of your business of more general interest. Pictures can also be effective.

(2) Twitter

The second most popular social medium is Twitter. It is said to have more than 320 million active users worldwide and is one of the top 10 websites in the United States. With Twitter, you can share short text updates of 140 or fewer characters, as well as videos, images, links, and more.

(3) Pinterest

Pinterest is a form of digital bulletin board where users can "pin" content. Users can create and organize their boards by category. For example, a user might have a board dedicated to travel pictures, another board dedicated to photography, and so on. Because each post must be an image or video it is a very graphic medium.

Pinterest's users are primarily women, and popular categories on the site are DIY projects, fashion, exercise, beauty, photography and food. It can be used for other applications but these applications use Pinterest most effectively.

(4) Instagram

Instagram is another offering of Facebook. Like Pinterest, Instagram is based entirely on photo and video posts. They boast of having over 400 million active users. Some of the more frequent postings are in categories such as travel, art, food, and fashion.

Instagram is designed primarily for the mobile user. It is largely a personal medium and is less effective in a business context.

(5) Tumblr

Tumblr hosts more than 200 million blogs, and its clientele skews young (half are under 25).

Tumblr is possibly the most difficult social media platform to use to boost a business. It is more versatile than some of the other platforms, allowing posts in several business formats. These include text posts, chat posts, quote posts, audio posts, photo posts and video posts. According to Business News Daily "As with Twitter, reblogging (reposting other users' content) is very quick and easy, so if a user with a lot of followers shares your content, it's possible to go viral fairly quickly. However, what sets Tumblr apart more than anything is its audience, which is less like a pool of users and more like one big tight-knit community full of smaller sub-communities."

e. Selling on Amazon and eBay

Should you have difficulty drawing people to your web site, have a limited number of products, and prefer not to have to pack and ship each item ordered, then you may want to look into platforms that do much of the work for you. One of the most popular is Amazon FBA.

(1) What is Amazon FBA?

Entrepreneur Magazine (https://www.entrepreneur.com/article/252685) suggests that "Amazon FBA (Fulfillment by Amazon) allows virtually anyone to sell their goods on the Amazon platform. Fulfillment is one of the biggest challenges of any ecommerce business. With FBA, Amazon will store your products in one of its warehouses, ship them to your customers, handle all refunds and returns and provide excellent customer service."

You still have responsibilities as a seller, but this system can allow you to rise above the everyday activities and replace that time with the higher level aspects of building a business. You still have to drive traffic to your product page and convert visits to sales.

With FBA you can also take advantage of Amazon Prime free shipping and other programs that are popular with customers. Not to be underestimated is the power of the Amazon brand. In addition, you can be sure that Amazon has worked hard to streamline the fulfillment process.

According to Josh Shogren of Passion into Paychecks (https://www.passioninto paychecks.com/my-amazon-fba-journey/), picking the right product is the key to success with FBA businesses: "It is vital that you spend a lot of time finding the right product that will give you the best chance for success."

Shogren suggests that some of the most important factors include:

- The price point of the product should be somewhere between $10 and $50.
- The product should be as light as possible.
- Check to see if any potential competitors have a 5,000 best seller rank (BSR) or lower in their primary category.
- Make sure there aren't any brand names within the product category or niche.
- If possible, sell a product that isn't easily broken.
- The more reviews a product has, the greater the competition is. Fifty or fewer reviews on first page

products is a good indicator that you can break into the market.

- The cost of manufacturing should be 25 percent or less of the actual sale price.

"Top Amazon sellers aren't like the rest," says Lauren Shepherd at Teikametrics (http://blog.teikametrics.com/2015/07/what-the-most-successful-fba-sellers-do-differently-webinar-recap.html) "The most successful sellers have adapted to the evolving ecosystem that is online retail by treating selling on Amazon like trading on the stock market."

According to Shepherd, the following six factors are crucial to your success:

- Scaling a business is easier when fulfillment logistics are handled by Amazon.
- Be willing to admit when you are wrong, and make adjustments accordingly.
- Manage your inventory, risk and cash flow.
- Focus on cash flow and access to working capital.
- Don't try to be right -- focus on making money instead.
- Measure your growth by quarters or years, not by weeks.

(2) Selling on eBay

According to eBay: "Why should I open an eBay Store?

Opening an eBay Store is the best way to help dedicated sellers maximize their online business. Sellers with an eBay

Store gain access to tools that enable them to develop their own brand and maximize sales.

Among the benefits:

- Customized design - Gain complete control over the look and feel of your Store (colors, graphics, content, etc.).
- Value listings - List items for lower fees and longer durations.
- Product organization – Use custom categories to organize and display your items.
- Buyer searches - Buyers can perform keyword searches within your Store.
- Cross-promotions - Control which of your other items are cross-promoted when buyers view, bid on, or win an item.
- Unique URL - Your Store has its own Web address (URL) that you can promote to buyers.
- Sales reports - Free sales and visitor traffic reports help inform your business strategies."

(3) Comparison

It is difficult to recommend one selling platform over the other because each is dependent on a number of factors. These can include how many products you offer, commissions on sales of your items, and similar considerations. For a general discussion of the differences between platforms see eBridgeConnections (http://www.ebridgeconnections. com/Media/Blog/June-2015/OUR-UNBIASED-COMPARISON-OF-AMAZON-AND-EBAY.aspx).

STUDY QUESTIONS

1. Why is the Internet such a powerful business platform?
2. Which of your business ideas best lend themselves to an Internet platform?
3. What are the major tools to develop increased viewership for your website?
4. What are the most commonly used social media?
5. What are some of the most important factors in online selling success?

STEP 3

Research the Market

Chapter Objectives:

On completing this chapter, you should be able to:

- Determine market research objectives for a prospective venture
- Collect meaningful and relevant demographic and market data
- Apply available information to the current project, recognizing its limitations and adapting it to the current situation
- Identify market segments, and develop an appropriate marketing plan
- Perform a break-even analysis

a. Market Research Fundamentals

Market research can be thought of as a three-part process:

(1) Determine what we need to know

Who are our customers? Where are they? How are they best reached?

What are they buying? From whom? Why? What are their price expectations?

How big is the market? How much is "up for grabs?"

How intense is the competition? What are their advantages/ disadvantages?

How is the product distributed, marketed? How are prices set and changed?

As an example of using these questions to gain greater focus and insight into a venture, let us consider a case with which the author has been closely acquainted since 1997. This case will be revisited several times within this text to build on the understanding developed, and to investigate the impact over time of the decisions made. While the case is set in southeast Louisiana, and the focus is on a wholesale distribution business, the lessons learned are widely applicable.

Mini-Case 3-1:   There is something basically wrong with our market research.

John and Alan Vinturella visited western St. Tammany parish (WST) in early 1997 to evaluate the feasibility of opening a branch of their family-owned plumbing supply firm based in Metairie, LA (suburban New Orleans). WST, 40 miles north of Metairie across Lake Pontchartrain, was a generally rural area, thought to have the potential to be an "exurb" of New Orleans in the future.

The parent firm, Southland Plumbing Supply, Inc., had been serving plumbing contractors in the greater New Orleans area for about 10 years at the time. Neither John nor Alan had ever been involved in a business startup, or the opening of a branch, before this.

The area investigated was in and around Covington and including Mandeville. Based on their study, they concluded that it was premature to open now. The local phone directory listed only 3 plumbing companies, the likeliest constituency for the proposed business. Discussions with principals of the three businesses were not encouraging; each managed to get what they needed delivered by remote supply houses, and local hardware stores stocked enough supplies to get them through an emergency. Only one of the plumbers was aggressively seeking to grow the business.

They visited the hardware store in town considered to have the best inventory of plumbing supplies, and these items did not appear to be a significant portion of their business. The store was buying from the same suppliers as the plumbers.

But their father insisted that the area was promising, and to re-think the issue. A "brainstorming" session led to some insight into what might have been wrong with their basic approach. John and Alan were applying their experience in Metairie to the Covington situation, when the differences rendered much of this experience inapplicable.

A supply house in Metairie, as in most urban markets, served only the "trade," that is licensed plumbing contractors, maintenance people, and public agencies. Should end users of plumbing products, or even intermediaries like builders, attempt to buy from a supply house, they would be referred to a tradesperson. In a rural market, with its smaller trade firms and more lax building codes, many people literally built their own homes, and the material was as likely to be bought by the homeowner, builder, or a handyman as by the trade.

In addition, Metairie was a "mature" market, where new residential construction was a relatively small component of supply house sales; much of the demand was for commercial construction and maintenance materials, and repair, replacement and renovation items for the area's aging housing stock. In contrast, Covington and nearby Mandeville formed a growing bedroom community, and most of the "action" was in new residential construction.

These observations emphasize that while the "numbers" are useful, they can lead to erroneous conclusions without a good feel for the nature of this type of business, and the characteristics of the specific market under consideration.

With these changes in their thinking, John crafted a new market research approach and continued his feasibility study. The potential sales volume was less a function of current population than of leading indicators, such as the rate of issuance of building permits.

Since permits included an estimated value of the finished house, and norms existed for the percentage attributable to plumbing materials, the dollar volume of plumbing supply sales in the area could be estimated. Applying an estimate of Southland's market share would then yield its expected sales volume. While the compounding of these estimates would yield a fairly wide range for expected sales, it would be indicative of the area's potential.

The branch would be basically a wholesaling operation, but retail sales would also be made. The customers would not be just plumbers, but everyone building a new home in the Covington-Mandeville area. Its product line would go beyond traditional plumbing items to include related homebuilding materials undersupplied to the area, such as septic tanks and water well equipment. Pricing would be competitive, but the added value of being a local operation allowed some flexibility. Traditional selling, almost exclusively supply house salespersons calling in person on plumbing contractors, would be replaced by advertising in the local "shopper" newspapers. The branch would locate on the main highway between Covington and Mandeville.

With this marketing plan, John could "run some numbers," and evaluate whether opening the branch made good business sense.

STUDY QUESTIONS

1. What do you think of John's marketing plan? Did he show a good grasp of who the customers are, and what they were looking for? Did he adequately assess the competition?

2. Was the Metairie experience with pricing applicable to the Covington analysis? Would you expect the margin in Covington to be better or worse?

3. Would it have been more prudent to start selling to the area from Metairie, watching its progress, and opening a branch a year later? Was the "window of opportunity" likely to close before then?

4. What are the longer-term consequences of becoming a wholesale/retail "hybrid?" Will this enhance or hinder the growth potential of the business? How will it affect the competitive situation? Are they entering a new business?

(2) Acquire the most current and relevant data available

There is a great deal of useful information only a "Google" search away. Industry directories and periodicals can give useful statistics, analyze trends, and provide projections. Trade associations and vendors can frequently provide data specific to the business you plan to enter. Universities, government offices, and chambers of commerce can frequently help with location-specific information. Census data is frequently rich in the kinds of information we need.

It is often difficult to convince prospective entrepreneurs to do a thorough job of market research. They are often unaware of how useful the information available can be, and of its relevance to their specific project. Consider the following examples:

Interested in opening a golf equipment store? According to the Economist (http://www.economist.com/blogs/ economist-explains/2015/04/economist-explains-1): "In 2006 some 30m Americans were golfers. But since then golf has hit a rough patch. And it is now struggling to attract a new generation of American players. In 2013, 160 of the country's 14,600 golf facilities closed, the 8th consecutive year of net closures. The number of players has fallen to around 25m."

As a $300 billion industry, home improvements and repairs currently generate about 1.8 percent of US economic activity—slightly below its decade-long average share. Harvard's Joint Center for Housing Studies (http:// www.jchs.harvard.edu/sites/jchs.harvard.edu/files/ jchs improving americas housing 2015 final.pdf) reported that: "By 2014 estimates, spending on homebuilding was less than 60 percent of its pre-recession levels, while spending on nonresidential construction had retraced less than 40 percent of its drop during the downturn. And while homebuilding is many years away from a full recovery, the home improvement industry could easily post record-level spending in 2015."

What does this have to do with the business of our choice? Directly, it shows market sizes and trends. Indirectly it can add to our level of sophistication about our industry, objectively confirm what we already knew, or challenge the assumptions on which we were going to base our plans.

Entrepreneurial Resources: Sample market research sources.

If we were going to consider opening a retail establishment, the Census (http://www.census.gov) is the richest source of data available. Some of its databases and tools are the following:

2010 Census Interactive Population Map
Use this tool to explore 2010 Census statistics down to the block level, compare your community with others, and embed charts on your web site.

American FactFinder
This interactive application provides statistics from the Economic Census, the American Community Survey, and the 2010 Census, among others.

Business Dynamics Statistics
This tool shows tabulations on establishments, firms, and employment with unique information on firm age and firm size.

Census 2000 EEO Data Tool

Select levels of geography based on residence or workplace. The estimates present information for various occupation groupings by race and ethnicity and sex.

Census Business Builder
Census Business Builder offers small business owners selected Census Bureau & other statistics to guide their research for opening or expanding their business.

DataFerrett
This tool is the analytical interface to TheDataWeb and allows users to create custom tables and data visualizatons, such as graphs and thematic maps.

Economic Database Search and Trend Charts
Easy access to Economic Statistics using drop-down menus. Create tables in ASCII text and spreadsheet format. Display customizable dynamic charts.

Industry Snapshots
These interactive pages present key statistics from the Economic Census with per capita ratios using data from Population Estimates for a selected industry.

Metropolitan/Micropolitan Population Map Viewer
A web-based interactive map application built to display demographic data at the Census 2010 tract level.

QWI Explorer

Provides detailed demographics; geographic (state, county, and metro/micro areas); ownership information; industry information, and recent and historical data.

QuickFacts
QuickFacts provides frequently requested Census Bureau information at the national, state, county, and city level.

For more localized data check with state and local agencies. States and localities differ as to how much data is available online. Departments of economic development are good places to start. Specific types of data that you may find useful include the following:

Public records
Sales tax collections, building permits, business incorporations

Trade associations
Real estate transfers, utility hookups

Trade journals for the industry you will be entering can be helpful.

Mailing lists may be purchased from InfoUSA (https://www. infousa.com/)

Exercise 3: **Market Research, Used-Book Store**

Assume you are planning to open a store to sell used books.

Identify the size of the industry and customer demographics.

(for 2004 data see https://are.berkeley.edu/~sberto/UsedBooks.pdf.

Find something more current)

Search business directories for data on firms in the industry.

Search computer databases and the Internet for relevant information.

List all sources used, whether or not they proved productive.

(3) Identify market segments

From our discussion of small business opportunities, we should have an idea of the general product area in which our business will compete. The next step is to clarify and refine the niche our business will fill, and this process is driven by information gathered on the opportunity.

A basic decision to be made is where in the process of satisfying consumer needs will our offering fall? The product delivery "chain" may be thought of as consisting of:

product manufacture, characterized by large competitors, a large initial investment, and the need for an effective distribution system;

wholesaling, a function currently undergoing some consolidation, and requiring sources of supply, and a dealer network;

retailing, a highly competitive area with a number of specialty niches, and;

services, generally the easiest types of businesses to start, but the hardest to get to a high level of profitability.

Individual businesses are generally identified in one of these categories, even if operating in a manner that falls between two of them, or that combines two or more.

Once the decision is made as to where in this spectrum our company will operate, our idea can take on a little more "shape," and we can begin the market research process. Frequently, the results of the market research cause us to reevaluate where in the product delivery process we will position our business (for discussion purposes, we will use the term product to include services).

Within the population of the prospective customers for our product (which could be a service), there are smaller groups, called market segments, with similar needs. Markets can be segmented along several different dimensions: product-related; geographic; "psychographic," or relating to traits, motives, and lifestyles; and demographic, relating to consumer age or income level.

Mini-Case 3-2:   How many piano tuners can this place support?

A piano tuner recently moved to Buffalo, NY, and would like to assess the business possibilities for him in his new home.

He plans to estimate how many piano tuners the greater Buffalo area can support, and compare that to the number listed in the phone book. How do we advise him as to how to estimate the "right" number of tuners for the area?

One approach is simply to guess. Would it be 1, 10, 50, or 100? Are you comfortable with this approach? I am not. An approach I would be comfortable with would be to search for data on estimates of how many piano tuners per capita there are in the U.S., and apply that ratio to the Buffalo area population (let's use 1.3 million). Is data on this likely to be available? Test your resourcefulness by trying to find it.

Assuming that data is not available, we must go to the "some assembly required" approach to estimating, that is, deriving the estimate from data which is available modified by related local and national data, norms, and "rules of thumb." While this seems as indirect as to be little better than just guessing, it can be a very useful exercise. If nothing else, it causes us to identify some important variables and how they relate to our business of interest. The inaccuracies of compounding estimates can be minimized by working in ranges to give us a "ballpark" figure.

How can I derive a meaningful estimate from generally available information? It would be interesting to know what percentage of American households own a piano, and how often they get it tuned. If the data is national, we may need to apply some local adjustment factor. Given the annual number of piano tunings, we can divide by the annual capacity of a tuner to determine how many are needed.

I will do an "off-the-top-of-my-head" calculation to illustrate the method, then leave it to you to provide real values:

Buffalo has about 400,000 households (population divided by 3 members on average); 8% of American households own pianos. I can think of no reason to apply any local adjustment to this figure, so we are talking about roughly 32,000 pianos. My guess is that two-thirds of all pianos are merely furniture, so that the remainder of about 11,000 is played regularly and in need of tuning. Tuners recommend that a piano be serviced twice a year, but my guess is that the average is probably once a year for active pianos, or 11,000 tunings per year.

A tuner can service 2 to 4 pianos a day; let us say 3 per day, 5 days a week, 50 weeks a year, or 750 tunings per year per tuner. To provide Buffalo's 11,000 annual tunings would require almost 15 tuners. The phone book lists 9. Sounds promising!

STUDY QUESTIONS

1. Is this a good approach? How many would you have guessed without this analysis? Does the result seem reasonable? Is it enough on which to base the opening of a business?

2. Could it have been done more scientifically? How? Would discussions with piano tuners and music

stores have been useful? Are there any journals worth consulting? Would a survey have helped?

3. Are pianos in places other than homes? Are there tuners not listed in the yellow pages?

The *Census of Retail Trade* provides the average number of stores per capita for a variety of retail outlets. Based on their data, we can determine how well our proposed market area is served on a relative basis for the type of business we plan to start. For example, there is, on average, a stationery store for every 33,000 people; for every 26,000 people there is one bookstore and one nursery and garden supply store. The population can presumably support a barber shop for every 2,200 residents, and a furniture store for every 3,000.

b. The Marketing Plan

With the information gathered in the research phase, we can refine our business concept further by considering our "marketing mix," those decisions to be made for our marketing plan that are generally referred to as the "four P's:" We will take a first pass at the following decisions to continue our screening, then refine the answers for the business plan.

(1) Product

What is the product that the market needs? How well positioned are we to provide it? How will we differentiate ourselves from the competition?

What brand name and packaging will we use? How wide will our product line be? What will be its features, accessories and options?

(2) Price

Will our price be competition-based or quality-image-based? What is the range of pricing options? How price-sensitive are sales? Can we be low cost <u>and</u> high service?

What will our terms be? What discounts and allowances will we provide?

(3) Promotion

How will we promote the product? What aspects of the product should we stress? How and where will we advertise? What are the most cost-effective media? Can we afford an agency?

Are there some non-traditional promotional methods which could be effective? Does our venture lend itself to personal selling over mass-marketing, cross-promotions with related products? Are there opportunities for free publicity?

(4) Place

Where and how will we distribute the product? What will the distribution "channel" look like?

Summary

Once a business idea is determined to be worthy of further consideration, we must assess its potential in detail. This is often an iterative process; as we select an approach to the market and do the necessary research, we may detect greater potential in a different approach and have to revise and repeat the research process. The first basic decision to be made is where in the product delivery chain we position ourselves. If there is a service that we expect to expand rapidly, we may choose to provide that service, or to supply some of the required materials to those who provide it, or even to manufacture some of the required materials.

With this decision made, subject to being revisited, we can design a research effort to assess the potential of this approach to the market. The first step is to determine what we need to know, that is what available information is the most meaningful in the measurement of the opportunity. Again the decisions are rather basic. What market will we serve? Who are our customers? What are they looking for? What is the competitive situation?

Strategic Internet searches can serve as a starting point. We can start with a "reconnaissance mission" to determine how much of what we would like to know is readily available. Often our market research objectives must be modified to use available information. In some cases, we may choose to survey the market to acquire data designed specifically to our needs. In every case, we must apply some judgment to the data, since we are trying to project our future prospects.

From the marketing research results, we must refine our marketing plan. What will our product be? What is our competitive advantage or distinctive competence? How will we price the product? How will we promote it? How will we distribute it?

Review Questions

1. Who are the most likely customers for the opportunities we discussed, i.e. the coffee shop and used-book store? What are they buying? What are their price expectations?
2. What would a good market research strategy be for each of these ventures? What would it be for a venture you may be considering?
3. What websites, periodicals and trade publications are available in these areas? What on-line search tools are available? How timely is the data? How applicable to your venture?

Mini-Case 3-3: Does anybody care how this stuff tastes? (Atlantic Brewing)

Jim Patton and Rush Cumming met at the Boston Brew Club, found out that they lived near each other on the Northshore, and began to carpool to meetings. Jim, a college professor, fancied himself quite the amateur brewmaster, and his home-brewed beers frequently won taste contests at the Club. Rush, a self-employed carpenter, was more interested in the tastings than the recipes, but enjoyed the conversations with Jim about the fine art of small-batch brewing.

It was an article of faith among members of such clubs, all over the country, that the products of the large commercial breweries were bland so as not to offend any of their mass clientele; greater emphasis was thought to be placed on shelf-life than on taste. By the mid-1980s, Jim and Rush were tracking with great interest the beginning of a new industry, the "microbrewery," where the techniques of home brewing were adapted to a minimal commercial scale.

Jim visited a microbrewery in Ohio, meeting the designer and builder of their equipment, an Englishman named Fred Glick, who had become something of a cult figure in the industry. Fred responded to Jim's interest in starting a microbrewery by roughing out a design that would meet Jim's specifications, and an estimate of the cost of building the state-of-the-art equipment.

On the flight home, Jim developed the outline of a business plan, and a rather detailed estimate of startup funds required. The funds were well beyond his means, but he and Rush could provide the seed money to prepare a private placement stock offering and present their story to prospective investors. Jim had already picked out the location of the microbrewery, near his home in Peabody, and a company name, *The Atlantic Brewing Company.*

The product was clear in his mind, a beer free of preservatives and made with a locally available spring water. They would produce a lighter brew, "Golden," and a heartier "Amber." Seasonal and specialty beers would also be made as production schedules allowed. Their products would be priced with imported beers, while offering greater quality and freshness. They would appeal to all premium beer drinkers, not just the connoisseurs.

Since the cost of bottling equipment was prohibitive, they would begin by distributing kegs only. This would require competing for tap space at bars and restaurants, initially on the Northshore with its affluent demographic, while attempting to develop a following in Boston area bars with college-student clienteles. They would distribute directly, delivering in company trucks.

Now all they needed were a few investors...

STUDY QUESTIONS

1. How would you rate the marketing plan? How is *Atlantic* differentiated from the competition? What need are they filling? Are we convinced that need exists?
2. Analyze their pricing strategy. What is their greatest competition?
3. Suggest a marketing campaign that emphasizes *Atlantic*'s strengths. To whom are we trying to appeal? What is the best way to reach them?

STEP 4

Check Feasibility

Chapter Objectives:

On completing this chapter, you should be able to:

- Make estimates of future performance
- Perform breakeven analyses

Breakeven Analysis

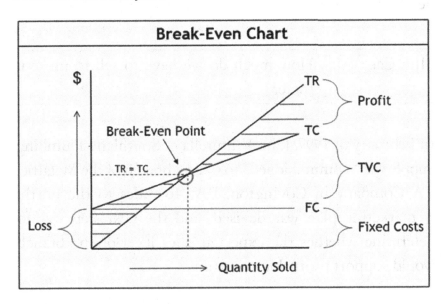

With a marketing mix determined, we can take our first look at the financial prospects for the venture. While many people are uncomfortable with the "guesswork" involved in projecting sales and expenses for a prospective business, there are approaches which at least yield *structured* guesswork, similar to the marketing research estimates earlier. In any case of predicting future events, there is no right *answer*, and if we are careful our judgment is as good as anyone's on our own business concept.

Breakeven analysis is a good way to develop a sense of the feasibility of a venture. It is a way to determine what level of sales is required to allow the venture to generate just enough "margin dollars" to cover its expenses. Margin is the amount of money left over after the cost of the goods sold is deducted. The process is best understood by example, and a continuation of the Southland Plumbing Supply case will be used:

Mini-Case 4-1:   How much do we have to sell to make it there?

In February of 1997, John Vinturella of Southland Plumbing Supply was "commissioned" to open a branch of the Metairie, LA Company in Covington, LA, 40 miles to the north. A marketing plan was devised, and the next step was to determine whether the expected sales level of the branch would support profitable operation.

From parish permit information, John estimated the amount of money to be spent on homebuilding and remodeling over the next year. Information from the Bureau of Labor Statistics allowed him to determine the percentage of that amount to be spent on plumbing materials. BLS data also provided an estimate of repair and replacement expenditures for existing homes.

After estimating the total amount of plumbing material sales in the market area, and analyzing the competitive situation, he assumed a 75% market share for the new branch (sound reasonable?). This yielded an expected sales figure, and from the ranges in his calculations, he decided on pessimistic and optimistic values for monthly sales (see following table).

John estimated that he would need two other people to adequately run the branch, a warehouseman and a delivery person. A delivery truck would be needed, and his new "car" would be a small pickup truck. Furniture requirements would be minimal, and shelving for inventory could be built inexpensively. Assuming that their trucks would be leased, he made the following estimate of monthly expenses:

EXPENSES

BREAKEVEN ANALYSIS

Salaries	John	$2,000	**Expenses**	$8,000	per month
	Others	$2,000			
	Benefits (25%)	$1,000	From Metairie Experience:		
Equipment	Trucks	$300	**Margin**	20%	per sales $
Leases	Other	$60			
Expenses	Transportation	$480			
	Insurance	$360	**Sales needed to generate expense $:**		
	Legal/Acctg	$150	Exp/Mar	$40,000	
	Utilities	$300			
	Supplies	$420			
	Advertising	$100	**Estimated sales**		
	Miscellaneous	$100	Low	$35,000	
Contingency	(10%)	$727	Expected	$45,000	
TOTAL		$7,997	High	$60,000	

Total expenses to operate the branch would be on the order of $8,000 per month. These are all essentially fixed costs, that is they are relatively constant within the estimated range of sales volume. Variable, or sales-volume-dependent, costs consist of only the cost of goods sold, estimated to be 80% of sales, based on the experience in Metairie.

The level of sales required to break even, then, is that sales volume at which the remaining 20% of revenues (margin) generates enough gross profit to pay expenses. In this case that number is $8,000/20%, or $40,000. This is below the estimate of the most likely sales volume, so there is a reasonable expectation of this being a profitable venture.

STUDY QUESTIONS

1. How would you rate the quality of the market research used to justify the venture? What would you have done differently? What would you have done additionally?

2. Given the information used in John's analysis, would you have opened the branch? Are they trying to justify opening the branch, no matter what the data showed?

3. Were John's expense estimates too rough? How could they have been refined? Were the expense categories reasonable and complete? Was the market share estimate realistic?

Let us now review the components of breakeven analysis in more general terms:

(1) Estimate monthly sales

If possible, it is better to "derive" a sales estimate than simply to pick one. For example, we may first try to find an estimate of the total demand for our product in our market area; market research will often yield a fairly well founded number for this, or provide norms which can be used.

Next an estimate of what share of that demand our company might reasonably be expected to capture can be multiplied by total demand to give the sales estimate. It is often useful to establish a sales range, for example, pessimistic, likely, and optimistic sales levels.

(2) Estimate monthly expenses

Identify the major expense categories for operating the business; SBA publishes a "Checklist for Going into Business," which contains some helpful worksheets. Make estimates of how much you would spend in each of those categories each month. Distinguish fixed costs from variable costs which depend on level of sales. Figure a total of monthly expenses. Estimate always on the conservative side. The natural tendency is to "cut too close" on expense figures, and the less visible costs such as permits and taxes are frequently overlooked. The above example missed one fairly basic expense. Have you figured which? How much should it have been? (Remember that these are 1977 dollars).

Note also in the example that 25% is added to the payroll figure for benefits. This might cover federal and state taxes, unemployment insurance, and sick and vacation time, but little else. If you plan to contribute to hospitalization insurance or educational costs, or other benefits, this figure should be increased accordingly.

The example also includes a figure for "Miscellaneous" expenses, and an added "Contingency" of 10% of total expenses. Is this enough to account for the omission?

(3) Calculate breakeven sales level

Determine your margin. For example, if you buy your product for $0.80 and sell it for $1, then $0.20 or 20% of each sales dollar is margin with which to pay expenses. If expenses are $8,000 per month, sales of $40,000 (20% of $40,000 is $8,000) represents a break even situation.

Many businesses deal in markup rather than margin. For example, if I buy a product for $0.80 and sell it for $1, I have marked it up $0.20, or 25% of my cost of goods. To minimize confusion, we will deal in margin rather than markup percentages.

(4) Compare and conclude

Where in our range of estimates does the breakeven sales figure fall? If it is above our optimistic estimate, prospects are grim. If it is around our expected figure, we may need to look a bit more closely. If it indicates that we can break even with a sales figure below our pessimistic estimate, or comfortably below our expected sales, it makes the cut.

Breakeven analysis is only a screening device, to help us sort out promising ventures from hopeless causes. We will discuss "serious" financial planning later, after we have chosen a prospective business for detailed analysis.

Once an opportunity passes the "screen test," we must then evaluate whether there might be an alternative to starting a new business. In some product areas, the chances for success are enhanced by acquiring a franchise. In some cases, purchase of an existing business can avoid the start-up trauma, while eliminating a competitor.

STEP 5

Consider Alternatives

Chapter Objectives:

On completing this chapter, you should be able to:

- Evaluate any advantage to working from home
- Compare a franchise to a traditional startup
- Value a company
- Buy an existing business

a. Work at Home Careers

A growing number of Americans are working from home. These include entrepreneurs and telecommuters for larger firms. Forbes (https://www.forbes.com/sites/kenrapoza/2013/02/18/one-in-five-americans-work-from-home-numbers-seen-rising-over-60/#905eb7e25c1d) reports that 30 million of us work from a home office at least once a week (2013 data). That number is expected to increase by 63% in the next five years, according to a study by the Telework Research Network (http://www.teleworkresearchnetwork.com). An estimated three million American professionals never step a foot in an office outside of their own home and another 54% say they are happier that way.

It is estimated (2012 data, https://www.businessforhome. org/2012/07/home-based-business-in-america/) that:

- A new Home Based Business is started every 12 seconds.
- 70% of Home Based Businesses succeed within 3 years versus 30% of regular businesses
- 44% of Home Based Businesses are started for under $5,000
- 70% of Americans would prefer to be self-employed
- $427 billion per year is made by Home Based Businesses

What has enabled this growth is the low cost of fitting out a home office. We can put together a premium personal computer with laser printer and scanner at a cost on the order of $3,000. With a high-speed Internet connection we can offer sophisticated services to consumers and to other businesses.

Think about what services you can offer online. First think freelance. Are you a skilled web developer? Do you have writing talent? Are you a creative graphics designer? Are you good at online research? Are you fluent enough to be a translator?

Work at home productivity is changing the way some industries deliver their products. Travel agents can now choose to work at home. Using a host agency for agent credentials and support as needed, the agent is self-employed while paying a portion of commissions to the host.

Do you want to sell products online? There are many sources of supply. *The Work at Home Woman* (https://www. theworkathomewoman.com/best-products-sell-home/) suggests a few with an emphasis on fashion. Here is one example:

"Featured in Vogue, Glamour, Lucky, and Tech Crunch, *Chloe + Isabel* is a social selling company that sells artisan designed jewelry. Jumpstart your own business for just $175. Merchandisers can earn 25% – 40% commission on all items sold."

If you do work at home, be aware of the disadvantages. Bayt (https://www.bayt.com/en/career-article-1601) outlines several of these:

Entrepreneurs working from home often feel isolation and loneliness. When they embark on their new career they realize how much they gave up socially from their previous job. They must find a way to stay in touch with their friends and also get feedback on their efforts.

They must have the discipline when they are "at work" to shield themselves from the distractions of the home environment. The home office setup should assist in separating home from office.

Similarly, the temptation to work longer and irregular hours is always there. In many cases the entrepreneur treats work at home in the same way as work in an office, working regular and reasonable hours and maintaining a satisfying work life balance.

b. Franchising

A franchise is a continuing relationship between a franchisor and a franchisee in which the franchisor's *knowledge, image, success, manufacturing, and marketing techniques* are supplied to the franchisee for a consideration. This consideration usually consists of a high "up-front" fee, and a significant royalty percentage, which generally require a fairly long time to recover.

Here are some statistics about the industry (http://www. azfranchises.com/quick-franchise-facts/):

- There are an estimated 3,000 different franchisers across 300 business categories in the U.S. which provide nearly 18 million jobs and contribute over $2.1 trillion to the economy.
- Franchises account for 10.5 percent of businesses with paid employees; almost 4% of all small businesses in the USA are franchises.
- It is estimated that the franchise industry accounts for approximately 50% of all retail sales in the US.
- The average initial franchise investment is $250,000- excluding real estate; the average royalty fees paid by

franchisees range from 3% to 6% of monthly gross sales.

Franchising offers those who lack business experience (but do not lack capital) a business with a good probability of success. It is a ready-made business, with all the incentives of a small business combined with the management skills of a large one. It is a way to be "in business for yourself, not by yourself."

Franchises take many forms. Some are simply trade-name licensing arrangements, such as *TrueValue Hardware*, where the franchisee is provided product access and participation in an advertising cooperative. Some trade name licenses, particularly in skin-care products, are part of a multi-level marketing system, where a franchisee can designate sub-franchisees and benefit from their efforts.

Others might be distributorships, or manufacturer's representative arrangements, such as automobile dealerships, or gasoline stations. It could be Jane's Cadillac, or Fred's Texaco; the product is supplied by the franchisor, but the franchisee has a fair amount of latitude in how the business is located, designed and run. The franchisor will frequently specify showroom requirements and inventory level criteria, and could grant either exclusive or non-exclusive franchise areas.

The most familiar type of franchise, however, is probably the "total concept" store such as McDonald's. Pay your franchise fee, and they will "roll out" a store for you to operate.

The advantages can be considerable. The franchise fee buys instant product recognition built and maintained by sophisticated advertising and marketing programs. The franchisor's management experience and depth assists the franchisee by providing employee guidelines, policies and procedures, operating experience, and sometimes even financial assistance. They provide proven methods for determining promising locations, and a successful store design and equipment configuration. Centralized purchasing gives large-buyer "clout" to each location.

The large initial cost can be difficult to raise. The highly structured environment can be more limiting than it is reassuring. Continuing royalty costs take a significant portion of profits. Several small business periodicals evaluate and rank franchise opportunities. There are now several franchise "matchmaking" firms who can assist in the evaluation process.

How do you choose among all the available franchises? Does it complement your interests? Even if you hire someone to manage the business, expect to spend a lot of time with the operation. Is the name well known? If not, what are you paying for? Is the fee structure reasonable, and all costs clearly described?

Is the franchisor professional? Evaluate them on the clarity of the agreement, and how well your rights are protected, the strength of their training and support program, and their commitment to your success. Be sure to talk to current franchisees about their experiences. Beware of a franchisor committed to a rate of growth that exceeds their ability to manage; they may not be sufficiently interested in the sales they have already made.

Is a franchise a sure path to instant riches? Is it the only hope for independent firms in today's market? Can Jerry's Quick Oil Change compete with SpeeDee? Does the franchise deliver business that we might not have gotten anyway? Is it really entrepreneurship; did I go into business or did my money?

Case Study 5-1   SpeeDee Oil Change of St. Charles Ave.

BACKGROUND

In 2008 Midas, the international brake service and automotive company bought the assets of SpeeDee Oil Change for $20.8 million. This ended over 30 years of growth and development of the SpeeDee brand and represented a significant cash out for its two owners.

Gary Copp and Kevin Bennett met at Loyola University of New Orleans in the 1970s as each pursued a business degree and considered future prospects. Both wanted to start a business at some point in the near future, and they kept in touch as each took a sales job on graduation.

Many of their get-togethers were spent brainstorming about business possibilities. Staying close to their personal interests, many of the opportunities they discussed related to automobiles or sports. As their ideas began to become more tangible with time, their attention was focusing more and more on servicing cars.

Kevin's uncle owned a service station on a busy corner in Metairie LA (suburban New Orleans), and had a little extra space to one side that was offered to them for a related use. It was decided to start a car wash as a "pilot project" in a sense for what they might want to do ultimately.

G&K Enterprises was formed to operate the car wash, and employees were hired so that Gary and Kevin could keep their "day jobs." A considerable amount of time was spent by both at the car wash, supervising, doing bookkeeping work, and watching and listening.

Though this venture consumed most of their spare time, they knew they were on the right track. Auto service stations were becoming largely self-service. Drivers, without attendants to check under the hood, could not tell when their oil was dirty, or know when it was time for some regular or seasonal service. Automobile warranties were getting longer, but requiring documentation that maintenance services were performed at prescribed intervals.

A market need had been created and, at the time, there was only one company with national aspirations performing the services that the gasoline stations had abandoned. Jiffy Lube had begun in the northeast U.S. and was setting the standard for the industry that G&K would enter. Jiffy offered these services with the added benefit of a 10-minute guarantee for an oil change, lubrication, and maintenance check. Based on owner's manual specifications, they would remind you of service intervals and requirements, and suggest other indicated maintenance procedures.

G&K sensed that it was still early enough for them to seize a leadership position in the industry. They converted their car wash into a quick oil change facility. A rolling oil can logo was developed and the name "SpeeDee" was chosen. Kevin still jokes that their 9-minute guarantee was not to one-up Jiffy, but to save SpeeDee money on a sign that was priced by the letter.

Their prototype was an instant success, and by the time they had opened three more outlets in the New Orleans area they realized they had a winner. Their profits allowed them to become full-time employees of the venture, and to package the SpeeDee Oil Change System (SOCS) for franchising.

GROWING PAINS

The company began to sell regional rights to sub-franchisors around the U.S. while maintaining the Gulf South region for themselves. Regions were tailored to the interests of prospective investors; early regions included New England, East Texas, and greater Los Angeles. Regional owners would then open stores or license franchisees throughout their franchise areas. These would all be new locations built to national specifications, unlike Jiffy's approach to achieve rapid growth by acquiring existing independents.

The SOCS strategy was to create a strong additional layer of co-entrepreneurs, the region owners, to become a national company in a short amount of time. By the late 1980s this strategy was beginning to take hold, but the cash demands on SOCS exceeded their expectations. They decided that they needed to direct more of their attention to developing their own region, the Gulf Coast, to improve their cash flow before returning to their national roll-out.

SPEEDEE ON THE AVENUE

There was one location in New Orleans that Kevin had always coveted for a SpeeDee outlet, St. Charles Avenue. To locals it is reverently referred to as "The Avenue;" a ride on the St. Charles streetcar is a recommended tourist attraction. In 1988, a location became available with the planned demolition of a seedy convenience store.

Unable to finance a company-owned shop at the site, Kevin offered a franchise on the property to a "drinking buddy," Al Serio. Al ran a very successful hardware store with his younger brother George, and was sufficiently well-heeled to finance the deal. Al asked Kevin for some time to discuss it with George and with their older brother Jerry, a successful computer consultant.

Al was not a very effective salesman in the meeting with his brothers. He could only do it if they joined him; he did not have the time or that much interest, but he felt obliged to Kevin. Jerry, whose schedule was a bit more flexible, said he would help if the others were interested, but it would not be his choice. George surprised his brothers by saying that he was a bit frustrated at being second-in-command at the hardware store, and that this might give him the opportunity to show his talents by being in charge of something.

George's comments turned the tide, changing the conversation from why they should not purchase the franchise to discussing the details of how they would run it. Al suggested a good candidate for shop manager under George's supervision. Jerry remembered an old friend in the auto parts business who could supply them and help with inventory control.

Al found out from his banker that their strong financial position would allow them to "borrow out," or finance the project entirely with debt. They would lease the land for $2,500 per month, borrow $200,000 secured by the building and equipment, and get a $100,000 credit line for franchise and start-up fees, and for working capital.

DECISION TIME

Kevin provided the Serios with some rather detailed expense information on the operation of a franchise. Jerry then factored in the financing details and developed pro-forma income statements for scenarios representing break-even, and expected and optimistic situations suggested by Kevin (see Attachment).

The general practice in the industry was to close only on Sundays; estimates were based on 26 sales days per month. Many outlets did as much business on Saturdays as on two weekdays.

The key income variables in the operation of the franchise are the number of cars serviced per day (called "rolls"), and the average invoice amount. The oil change is basically a break-even proposition generating about a $25 ticket. To succeed, an operator has to generate enough add-on sales, such as tune-ups and radiator flushes, to double the average ticket.

The key expense variable is payroll cost, viewed as a percent of sales. This is controlled not by paying low salaries, but by keeping the shop busy, thereby spreading a basically fixed cost over a larger sales figure. The more successful outlets kept their payroll costs on the order of 20%.

The traffic-count for the location was excellent, about 50% higher than what was considered the threshold for a SpeeDee outlet; this suggested that they should have little trouble meeting a target of 40 rolls per day. The location is in the commuting pattern for the prosperous uptown part of the city, about three-quarters of the way downtown. The surroundings were a moderately busy commercial area on St. Charles, with generally low-income housing off The Avenue.

Attachment: Pro-Forma Monthly Income Statement

SpeeDee Oil Change	ST. CHARLES AVENUE			
	Days	26	26	26
	Cars/Day	36	40	45
	AvgInvoice	$41.82	$50.00	$52.00
		BrkEven	*Expected*	*Optimistic*
Net Sales		$39,144	$52,000	$60,840
Cost of Sales	25.0%	$9,786	$13,000	$15,210
GROSS MARGIN		$29,358	$39,000	$45,630
		======	=======	=======
Payroll w/Taxes (% of Sales)		26.6%	22.0%	19.0%
		$10,425	$11,440	$11,560
Occupancy (Land/Bldg/Tax)		$5,075	$5,075	$5,075
Franchise Costs		$5,872	$7,800	$9,126
Advertising	10.0%	*$3,914*	*$5,200*	*$6,084*
Royalties	5.0%	*$1,957*	*$2,600*	*$3,042*
Insurance		$1,156	$1,220	$1,264
Garage/General/WkComp		*$960*	*$960*	*$960*
Damage Claims	0.5%	*$196*	*$260*	*$304*
Services		$2,052	$2,168	$2,248
Bank, Misc. Fees		*$700*	*$700*	*$700*
CredCd Discount	0.9%	*$352*	*$468*	*$548*
Shop Services		*$1,000*	*$1,000*	*$1,000*
Office Expense		$955	$955	$955
Shop Expense		$900	$900	$900
Debt Service		$2,923	$2,923	$2,923
TOTAL EXPENSES		$29,358	$32,481	$34,050
PROFIT/LOSS		$0	$6,519	$11,580

While franchising is often billed as a safe path to riches, an increasingly vocal group of critics, including several franchisee associations, are warning prospective franchisees to beware. "The problem isn't that franchising is a bad concept," said Robert Purvin, chairman of the American Association of Franchisees and Dealers. "It's that franchising has become such a seller's market that many people are buying into bad systems."

c. Buying an Existing Business

If a franchise for our chosen opportunity is not feasible, our other alternative to starting a business is to buy an existing business. To some extent, buying a business is less risky because its operating history provides meaningful data on its chances of success under our concept. We must, however, balance the acquisition cost against what the cost of a startup might have been.

One important factor is the seller's reasons for offering the business for sale. Often these are for personal and career reasons, such as a readiness to retire with the absence of a successor, or another opportunity perceived as a better fit. Where there are business reasons for selling, such as personnel problems, or inability to stand up to the competition, we must decide whether all that is missing is a quality of management that we can provide, or that there are some changes we can make in the way the business is operated that will make the difference.

Due diligence must be performed before a binding offer is made. Is the company's history and network of business relationships clear? Are their financial statements representative? What do they say about the business? Are there any unstated dangers or risks? Are there any hidden liabilities? Often, a review of the financials by our banker and accountant can be valuable.

How "good" an organization is it? How is it perceived by its customers and suppliers? If we do not buy it, how tough a competitor will it be? What will be the effect of an ownership change on the customer base, supplier relations, etc.? How much customer loyalty is to the business, and how much to the current owner?

Does the company have a "niche?" Is it the one in which you want to operate? Is there a competitive advantage to the operation that is sustainable? Are its assets useful to you? Will key personnel remain with the business?

If the decision is made that purchase of an existing business could improve our chances for success, we must then evaluate existing businesses to determine whether any are available at a price that is economically more favorable than a new venture. How do we value a business?

Before examining specific techniques for business evaluation, it must be emphasized that there is no one correct value for a business. Any valuation is based on assumptions, and projections of future performance. As in our breakeven analysis discussion, discomfort about basing financial decisions on assumptions and projections is natural.

Entrepreneurship requires exploring uncharted territory, and operating in an environment of uncertainty. Success depends on applying our best judgment to reducing that uncertainty.

Mini-Case 5-1:   Are personal computers just a passing fad?

Clay Olson was interested in opening a retail computer store in Charlotte, NC in 2013. He had a good location, next to his furniture store, and good buying power with a computer distributor. His cash position was strong and the furniture part of the operation had good banking relations with considerable borrowing power.

His inclination was to buy an existing store, and move it to the furniture store building. One day an ad in the newspaper's "Business-to-Business" listings caught his eye. A small computer retailer/assembler was listed by a local business broker. Clay read the package given him by the broker, and requested a meeting with the owner.

Clay found the owner, Sam Romer, difficult to read. Sam was an interesting character, 30-ish with a hint of a foreign accent and a "know-it-all" demeanor. By his account, he had the buying connections to purchase high-quality components from little-known manufacturers, and that he and his technician would then assemble and fine-tune them. Their competitive advantage was then that they could sell high-performance computers for the price of "off-the-shelf mediocrities."

The customer list, oriented toward university and government users, was very impressive. There was no established marketing program, and little company recognition outside the customer list. Many of their sales were attained by competitive bid, generally several units at a time with small profit margins. Financial records were very disorganized, and Clay noticed that the company, which had earlier been incorporated as ByteWyse, Inc., had recently been converted into a sole proprietorship.

Sam seemed to have a good grasp of the technical aspects of the business, and a confidence-building if not completely likeable sales manner. He offered as his reason for selling that he wanted to return to graduate school, and that he could continue to sell for the buyers on a commission basis. If Clay chose not to use him, Sam would sign a one-year non-compete agreement. The technician, a real "hacker," was willing to stay on to do purchasing and system assembly for the new owners.

The sale price was $75,000; Sam valued the equipment and inventory at about two-thirds of that.

The equipment seemed to be current and well-kept, and the inventory was well organized. Clay would then be paying about $25,000 for the customer list and purchasing relationships. He asked Sam for about a week to think about it before returning for further discussion.

STUDY QUESTIONS

1. Does Clay have enough information to make an offer? What else should he do? Is there any one with whom he should consult for advice?

2. How do you feel about the "intangibles?" Are you satisfied with Sam's reasons for selling the business? How do you feel about keeping him on as a salesman?

3. What exactly is Clay buying? Is he likely to retain existing customers? Could he not establish similar buying relationships anyway? Should he keep the technician?

4. Does the company give Clay a "running start" in the business? Does it offer a better foundation for growth than a start-up? Is it limiting in any way?

5. Should Clay make a lower offer? Based on what? For how much? What should his negotiating strategy be?

d. Business Valuation

Small-business sales are generally (on the order of 94%) sales of assets, with no assumption of liabilities; the remainder are sales of company stock. Often the seller finances part of the purchase (see Figure 5-1); typically the buyer makes a down payment on the order of one-third of the sales price, with repayment terms of five years at market rates. Do you see any danger for the seller in financing the sale?

The most difficult issue in small business sales is establishing a selling price. It is an inexact science, characterized by a seller's too-high expectations, and an overly skeptical prospective buyer.

We will consider three basic methods of evaluating a business: a market approach; a book-value approach; and, an earnings approach.

The market approach is the simplest method, basing the value of the business on projections of earnings multiplied by a typical price/earnings ratio for the industry. While this technique is often applied to transactions involving publicly-traded companies, it is seldom applicable to the small closely-held company. There is a ready market for a few shares of a public company, but small businesses are not so easy to "turn-over," and their generally local nature makes them more vulnerable to economic cycles. Financial practices and reporting are also generally less consistent in smaller businesses than in the larger ones on which most industry-wide averages are based.

These inconsistencies cause most business valuators to "re-cast" the financial statements of closely-held companies. For many of these firms, earnings are understated; whereas larger firms try to maximize profits, the objective of most smaller firms is to minimize taxes. How is this strategy implemented? While the vast majority of small businesses

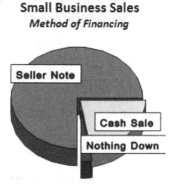

Small Business Sales
Method of Financing

Figure 5-1

use aggressive but clearly ethical methods, opportunities exist for abuse.

Owners can manipulate family member salaries based on the relative advantages of paying personal versus corporate taxes. They can pay family members who do not really work there. Personal expenses could be charged to a company account. Assets could be understated, and/or liabilities overstated. In businesses which make a lot of cash sales, some could be made without invoices, with the owner "pocketing" the proceeds. Are these practices illegal? Are they unethical?

We will now outline the more commonly applied methods of valuation, then illustrate them with a case study.

(1) Earnings

The earnings approach to valuing a business views the business as one more option for investing our money, that is, given our assessment of the risk involved, we have a certain expectation of return. We would certainly expect a greater return than on securities backed by the U.S. Treasury, but would possibly accept a lesser return than on a highly speculative venture.

Let us say that we have an opportunity to buy a business for $240,000 that projects annual earnings of a little over $40,000. This is an annual return on investment of about 18%, based on the owner's projections. Let us say further that it is a stable, mature business with a clear financial history and relatively little risk. Is 18% return satisfactory? It depends largely on the quality of the projections, and alternative investment possibilities.

Is the owner's projection likely to be objective? What are alternative methods of projecting earnings? Are economic conditions consistent enough for a historical average to be meaningful?

Are there any "dark clouds on the horizon" for the market area, or for the industry? What is the competitive situation? How is the business' market share? What are the long-term prospects for a small independent company in this industry?

Are last year's earnings a good indicator of earnings for the next few years? Were there any unusual circumstances? Are they likely to be repeated? Can we make a better estimate? What will we base it on? What is the quality of the financial records? Are there useful trade sources?

Could earnings be improved when we take over? Do we see waste, overpayment for materials or services, excess or excessively paid employees? How does the owner's pay and perquisites compare to our "opportunity cost," that is, the amount we could earn elsewhere?

Could earnings not be as good as they seem? Is equipment in disrepair or space insufficient? Will key employees leave the company? Will they be committed to a new owner? Will a major customer be lost? Are key buying relationships assured? Is company reputation an asset or liability?

Are there better investments available, without the everyday worries of business ownership? Do we prefer the business owner lifestyle to passive investment?

(2) Book Value

The book-value of a corporation is generally shown on its balance sheet as "Net Worth," or "Owner's Equity." It represents the excess value of the company's assets over its liabilities. What is implied in accepting this value as a sales price? It assumes that all components of the balance sheet are fairly valued, and that the assets are useful to the new owner's mission. Book-value sales are almost always based on adjustments to the balance sheet. What do we look at more closely?

Balance sheet items that are generally deserving of closer inspection include:

CURRENT ASSETS:

Accounts Receivable: How current are they? Discount by age.

Notes Receivable: How collectable are they? What are the payment terms?

Inventory: Is it counted correctly? How is it costed?

Is allowance made for overstock and obsolete items?

LONG-TERM ASSETS

Depreciation is a tax device, applied as aggressively as the law allows.

Assets should be revalued in their current state, by market or replacement value.

The seller may want to keep, and the buyer not want to buy, some assets.

How do we verify the adjustments? We may need to take inventory ourselves, and to have professional appraisals of the physical assets. This is not to say that the conscientious buyer cannot sometimes still be misled.

Other variations on the process might be where the buyer would pay adjusted book value plus 2 or 3 years' earnings, or might buy only selected assets. Frequently the selling price can vary depending on the terms, such as the amount of seller financing, years to repay, and interest rate.

As an example of this evaluation process, let us take another look at the Covington, LA plumbing wholesale operation:

Case Study 5-2   Tammany Supply, Inc. (A)

BACKGROUND

In February of 1997, John Vinturella of Southland Plumbing Supply was "commissioned" to open a branch of the Metairie,

LA company in Covington, LA, 40 miles to the north. John selected a location on Highway 190, the main road between Covington and Mandeville and the business thoroughfare for all of western St. Tammany parish (county). The site was just across Lake Pontchartrain from Southland's main operation, via world's longest bridge, the Causeway.

"Buck" Rogers, a good young warehouseman at Southland, was assigned to run the Covington warehouse. John hired a local truck driver in the last week of February, and they began to stock the branch from out of the Metairie inventory. The highly visible location paid off immediately, as several sales were made during the stocking process to passers-by.

Sales comfortably exceeded the breakeven estimate of $40,000 per month. Operating for essentially 10 months of 1997, sales averaged almost $50,000 per month and seemed to be accelerating before the typical seasonal slowdown from December to February.

VALUING THE BRANCH

In early 1998, John and his family began to discuss "spinning-off" the branch as a separate corporation, with John trading his partial ownership of Southland for complete ownership of the Covington operation (working title "Tammany Supply, Inc.").

In March 1998, Southland's accountant worked up a 1997 income statement for the Covington branch as if it had operated independently. She also, with John's input, projected the following three years' performance for valuation purposes. To complete the picture, she projected the value of the Covington assets on June 30, 1998, the day the sale would take place.

All that remained was to determine a selling price that John would find worth paying, and the accountant would consider in Southland's best interest. To insure fairness to all parties, it was decided that it would be an "arm's-length" transaction, that is, that John would pay a fair market price.

Southland would finance the inventory for one year, but the remainder of the sale would be cash. John could apply the value of his Southland stock, he would sell some real estate he owned, and borrow the rest from the bank.

Following is the statement presented to John by the accountant:

Tammany Supply, Inc.						
Income Statement	Actual	>>>>>	>>>>>		>>>>>	Projected
	1997	1998	1999		2000	
Sales	496486	660000	720000		800000	
Cost of Goods Sold	394763	528000	576000		640000	
	20.5%	20.0%	20.0%		20.0%	Margin
Total Income	101723	132000	144000		160000	
		1.33	1.09		1.11	SalesIncr
Expenses:		0.98	0.95		0.92	EconScale
Personnel	42058	54791	56784		58046	

Tammany Supply, Inc.						
Income Statement	Actual	>>>>>	>>>>>		>>>>>	Projected
Operations	13041	16989	17607		17998	
Sales	6557	8542	8853		9050	
Administration	9225	12018	12455		12732	
Depreciation	2074	2702	2800		2862	
Total Expenses	72955	95043	98499		100687	
						AvgProfit
Profit/Loss BIT	28768	36957	45501		59313	$42,635

The grayed areas in the statement represent the assumptions on which the figures were based. The sales increase row shows a 33% increase in the first full year (20% due to having 12 rather than 10 sales months), followed by 9% and 11% gains in subsequent years. With each sales increase, expenses are increased proportionately, "deflated" slightly by the economy-of-scale factor. A 20% margin is assumed throughout the three projected years.

But John knows of some ways in which expenses would have differed if the branch had been truly independent, and that the proper adjustments would present a more accurate picture of expenses as his company.

In particular, the branch was charged for $2,000 of a clerical assistants' time for things that his staff will now do themselves. In addition, the branch was not charged for supplies, and a small percentage increase in each expense category should be allocated to cover that. With these adjustments, a revised expense section of the income statement would be:

Expenses:	Adjust 1997		1998	1999	2000	
Personnel	-2000	40058	52186	54083	55285	
Operations	5.0%	13693	17839	18487	18898	
Sales	2.0%	6688	8713	9030	9231	
Administration	5.0%	9686	12619	13078	13368	
Depreciation		2074	2702	2800	2862	
Total Expenses		72199	94058	97479	99645	
						AvgProfit
Profit/Loss BIT		29524	37942	46521	60355	$43,586

EARNINGS APPROACH

The average profit over one actual and three projected years will be the basis for valuation by the earnings approach. Let us look at desired returns of 16, 18 and 20%:

Earnings = Investment * Return on Investment, or
Investment = Earnings ($43,586) / Return (16,18, or 20%)

If we require a return of 20% on our investment, this level of earnings justifies a selling price of $217,930. Should we be able to live with 16%, we could pay $272,413. Let us settle on an 18% return, suggesting a value of $242,142, and look at other valuation methods.

BOOK VALUE

Since the transaction would be an asset purchase, let us look at the asset section of the balance sheet prepared by the accountant:

Assets:	1998
Cash	22831
Accounts Receivable	85800
Collection Days	37.17
Inventory	118411
Turns	5.44
Other Assets	11733
Total Assets	$238,775

Again, John is aware of adjustments that should be made to make the statement more accurate. He suspects that about $4,000 of the accounts receivable is uncollectible, and that inventory is about $6,000 overexpressed. He also estimates that the fixed assets of the business have been depreciated to about $8,000 less than their replacement value. Adjusted book value is then:

Assets:	1998	Adjust
Cash	22831	
Accounts Receivable	81800	-4000
Collection Days	37.17	
Inventory	112411	-6000
Turns	5.44	
Other Assets	19733	8000
Total Assets	$236,775	

COMPOSITE

The market approach is not very appropriate here, since the characteristics of such a small firm are so much different from those for which price/earnings ratios would be reported. The large plumbing supply chains report p/e's of 8.5 to 12 on after tax earnings. A 20% tax rate on average earnings ($43,586), would leave $34,868; assuming a p/e for a small firm of 7, the market approach would yield a value of $244,076. Generally, in valuations of this type, some composite of the earnings value ($242,142) and adjusted book ($236,775) is used. In this case, they are so close that it seems safe to use $240,000 as a fair market value.

STUDY QUESTIONS

1. Is John underestimating the disadvantages of independence: decreased purchasing power; loss of access to the considerably larger inventory in the Metairie warehouse, and; management depth and other synergies due to being part of a larger operation?
2. Can John assume that Southland's customers will become Tammany's customers? Why would they, or why might they not? Can TSI maintain the service level they had with Southland's resources behind them?
3. John is 35 years old, and knows the administrative side of the business, but not the "pieces and parts;" Buck knows the material but now, at 20 years old, has become purchasing agent as well as warehouse manager. Are they in over their heads?

4. Is an arms-length transaction feasible when the buyer has so much more information than the seller? Is John's suggested price going to be acceptable?

5. Could the final price have been flexible, based on the first few years' performance of TSI? Should John have factored in the cyclical nature of the business, rather than counting on steady growth for the evaluation period?

6. Do you agree with the evaluation process? What might you have done differently? Do you agree with the result? If you were to modify it, in which direction would you go? Should the deal happen? Is it "win-win?"

e. Negotiating the Sale

If we decide we want to buy a business, we should decide on a bargaining range before we go into the final negotiating session. If we cannot meet on price, perhaps concessions on payment terms could make up the difference. We should know the tax and legal consequences of our options. If the discussion takes us outside our range, we should schedule another session, and reanalyze the data. We must allow for the possibility that the deal cannot be made.

Ultimately we must decide whether the purchase, at a price that the seller will accept, gives us a better chance of success than starting from scratch in competition with the business. Perhaps the seller's errors would start us in a deficit position; we might prefer creating our own corporate culture and customer relationships; maybe we can find a better location, facility, newer equipment, etc. On the other hand, the cost of taking sufficient business away from existing firms could be ruinous.

What franchises are available in these areas? Have you patronized any similar business which might form the basis for your venture?

With a marketing plan in place, we can refine our consideration further by beginning to make the very tangible decisions that allow us to test the feasibility of the venture. How many people will we need? What will we have to pay them? How much space will we need? What is it likely to cost? What are our equipment needs? What other operating expenses will there be?

What are our sales expectations? How do expenses vary with the level of sales? What level of sales will lead to a breakeven operation? How likely are we to achieve this level? How long will it take?

Once we have identified a venture where the answers to these questions indicate promise, we must consider the alternative ways to seize the opportunity. We can choose to start a new business "from scratch," acquire a franchise, or purchase an existing business. The cost of bringing a new business to profitability must be compared to the higher expenses but potentially surer path to success of franchising, and to the purchase price and potential of an existing business.

Establishing the purchase price of a "going concern" can be particularly difficult. While there are alternative methods to quantifying a value from available data on the firm, the quality of that data is often suspect because it is provided by the seller.

Case Study 5-3	Tammany Supply, Inc. (B)

INTRODUCTION

Based on evaluations done by Southland Plumbing Supply, verified and fine-tuned by John Vinturella, John bought the assets of Southland's Covington, LA branch from his father and two brothers in mid-1998. Tammany Supply, Inc. was formed in June 1998, to begin operating on July 1, the effective date of the sale.

The branch had opened in early 1997 (see the "A" case), and had moderately exceeded expectations. In the spring of 1998 the business was evaluated, and a consensus was reached on a selling price of $240,000.

To pay for the branch's inventory, which represented about half of the sale value, John would apply his $65,000 worth of stock in the parent company and Southland would finance the remaining $55,000 over two years at market interest rate. For the other half of the sale value, John would pay $35,000 cash (from proceeds of the sale of some property he owned in Metairie), and pledge the $85,000 in accounts receivable to Southland. This would be paid monthly, as collected, with the remainder paid out in full at the end of the third month, collected or not.

While the terms may seem complicated, this structure was necessary to allow John to make the purchase. At 35 years old, John was risking all the assets he had accumulated in 12 years of working and investing, and any future inheritance (cashing in his Southland stock) on the success of TSI. Most of the remaining proceeds from the sale of the Metairie property were used for a down payment on a house in Covington, and a working capital loan to TSI ($25,000).

John's only other asset was his one-third ownership in the building in which TSI would operate. It was a former truck-repair garage that had been foreclosed on by an area bank; after a few months of renting the building, Southland was offered an attractive purchase price and terms by the bank. Instead, John and his brothers decided, for tax reasons, to form a partnership to buy it outside the corporation.

After receiving assurance from the bank that his credit history and the equity in the building supported his assuming the entire loan, John approached his brothers about a buyout. The building had appreciated some and was generating some income, requiring compensation in addition to assuming their share of the loan. They agreed on an amount, and with its payment John was now the sole owner of the building and its accompanying loan.

John unlocked the doors of TSI at 7am on July 1, 1998, hoping some customers would show up. He was in debt a half-million dollars, and his only chance of ever climbing out was to sell a lot of pipe and fittings.

START-UP TRAUMA

The long work-week required in serving the building trades was made even longer by having to catch up the administrative backlog after hours. For ten hours a day during the week and Saturday mornings, John was selling, serving customers, and directing warehouse and delivery operations. After hours, on Saturday afternoons, and frequently on Sundays, he was making bank deposits, paying bills, billing customers and making collection calls, writing purchase orders, and analyzing what was happening.

He had hired Bill, 10 years his senior, as a salesman but found he needed operations help more. Bill made the transition nicely, taking over purchasing as well as supervising the warehousemen. Bill would occasionally make outside sales calls, but increasing sales volume was less of a problem than servicing the customers that had already come to rely on TSI. Soon after, John hired Harry, 20 years his senior, to help with counter sales and bookkeeping.

With the added hands, and accompanying maturity, John could finish most of his work during working hours, and finally felt comfortable taking an occasional day off. Still, by 2000 John had not taken a real vacation since starting TSI, and it was time to assess where the business was headed and the best way to get there.

FIRST THREE YEARS

Sales comfortably exceeded expectations for the first three years as TSI (see Figure 5-2).

By the end of 2000, John had paid off TSI's debts to Southland and to himself, and was beginning to draw a nice salary. The size of the staff had doubled since opening in 1998, and formed a hard-working and harmonious team. TSI was exceeding all the performance norms for the industry.

The company had decided on a March 31 fiscal year end, so income for 1998 has been annualized (it was a 9-month fiscal year). Also, for each year indicated, year-end actually includes the first quarter of the following year. This year-end was chosen to coincide with the end of a traditionally slow period, greatly simplifying taking physical inventory on over 6,000 items.

Following is a summary of financial performance for the period:

The performance improvements over projections were due largely to TSI's broadening its concept of the plumbing supply customer from plumbing contractors only to the general public. Direct-to-user (DTU) sales are unpopular with contractors, but improved sales volume, and the higher margins of retail sales make them worth the criticism to a supply house.

Tammany Supply, Inc.

First 3 Years Performance

Balance Sheet, End of 1980

	Income, 1998-2000			
	TOTAL	PROJECTED	Assets: Current	$307,576
			Assets: Other	$102,327
			TOTAL ASSETS	$409,903
Sales	$3,727,486	$2,180,000		
Gross profit	$943,094	$436,000	Liab.: Current	$84,689
As % of sales	25.3%	20.0%	Liab.: Long-Term	$60,133
Pretax income	$266,501	$144,818	Equity	**$265,081**
As % of sales	7.1%	6.6%	TOTAL LIAB/EQ	$409,903

MOVING TO THE NEXT LEVEL

By 1980, John found it necessary to expand and improve TSI's space. Building economies of scale were such that he tripled the size of the building, bringing in tenant companies in related but non-competitive businesses (carpeting, paint, appliances).

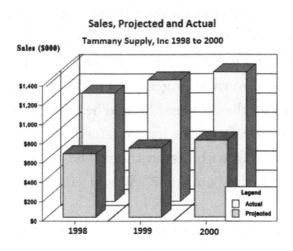

Figure 5-2

113

TSI became a distributor of Kohler plumbing products, the best in the industry (they had been buying Kohler indirectly through Southland before then). They built a state-of-the-art showroom, and began to advertise on local television. The warehouse was remodeled, and a mezzanine added. A fork-lift and new truck were purchased. The company also purchased FACTS, a software package tailored to wholesale operations.

St. Tammany Parish was booming, and TSI was gearing up to service that boom. Two regional plumbing supply chains offered to buy the business, but John was not interested. One opened a small Covington branch in competition with TSI, but it barely lasted a year.

STUDY QUESTIONS

1. Was the purchase agreement with Southland really at "arm's length," or were concessions made to John that might not have been made to an outsider? Did the terms lower the effective selling price? Was Southland continuing to bear some of the risk of TSI's success?

2. Was John overreaching his financial resources when he purchased the business? Should he have postponed the deal a year? Should he have retained the partnership in the building with his brothers? Did he leave himself any financial "cushion?" Would you have done the same?

3. How do you explain the way in which performance exceeded projections? Was one year of operating

experience enough to project sales for the next three years? Did John "lowball" his sales estimates to Southland? Should John offer a supplemental payment to Southland? Could John's actions as business owner been enough different from his actions as partner to explain the difference in performance?

4. Are two years of growth and success (mid-1998 to mid-2000) enough to justify the large additional investment made in 2000? Should it have been done more stage-wise? Is the observed growth rate sustainable? What are the consequences of it not being? Discuss in terms of company investment, and John's personal investment (building expansion).

5. What are the implications of the competition "discovering" the Covington market? Have any barriers to entry been erected? Why could TSI drive a larger competitor out of the market? After they left, do you think they had given up on the market entirely?

STEP 6

Write a Business Plan

Chapter Objectives:

On completing this chapter, you should be able to:

- Develop *pro-forma* financial statements that provide quantitative targets for progress
- Define a business opportunity in the widely-accepted and easily recognized Business Plan format
- Use the preparation of the plan to refine the concept, detect gaps and weaknesses, and anticipate the questions of prospective stakeholders.
- Produce a highly professional and meaningful plan that can serve to guide the implementation process
- "Sell" your project and plan to prospective stakeholders and your "support structure" of family, banker, accountant, *etc.*

a. Business Planning Overview

The purpose of a business plan is to recognize and define a business opportunity, describe how that opportunity will be seized by the management team, and to demonstrate that the business is feasible and worth the effort. Where implementation of the plan requires participation of lenders and/or investors, the plan must also clearly and convincingly communicate the financial proposal to the prospective stakeholders: how much you need from them, what kind of return they can expect, and how they can be paid back.

Many entrepreneurs insist that their business concept is so clear in their heads that the written plan can be produced after start-up; this attitude "short-circuits" one of the major benefits of producing the plan. "A realistic business plan might save you from yourself by persuading you to abandon a bad idea while your mistakes are still on paper," says Roger Thompson in *Nation's Business*.

Do many people need to be saved from themselves? Are many entrepreneurs so determined to go into business that they overlook or underestimate the potential pitfalls? Is that all bad? Can many business proposals stand the harsh light of skepticism?

Let us say we worked out the numbers on paper, and are convinced that our plan is sound. Do we still need to write the plan? The discipline of writing a plan forces us to think through the steps we must take to get the business started, and, to "flesh out ideas, to look for weak spots and vulnerabilities," according to business consultant Eric Siegel. A well-conceived business plan can serve as a management tool to settle major policy issues, identify "keys to success," establish goals and check-points, and consider long-term prospects.

Who is the audience for it? Certainly, the plan is very useful if we are looking for investors or lenders. It is the primary tool used to convince prospective stakeholders that the idea is promising, the market is accessible, the firm's management is capable, serious and disciplined, and that the return on investment is attractive. But even if we can finance the venture ourselves, these are useful issues to address.

What are the elements of a good business plan, and how does it differ from a bad one?

The appearance of the plan says something about its preparers. It should be professional, though not lavish, so as not to distract from its contents.

While the formats of business plans can be as varied as the businesses themselves, there are components that should appear in all plans. These include an executive summary, elements which describe the opportunity, elements which specify how the business will operate, an analysis of financial expectations, a closing summary, and any supporting documentation.

Let us discuss each of these in a little more detail, with an audience assumed to be a reader who might be a prospective investor or lender, a trusted professional advisor, or a friend whose business judgment we value.

(1) "Packaging"

The cover and title page should contain company name, address, phone number, primary contacts, and the month and year of issue. Often, the issuers include a copy number to control circulation.

The executive summary introduces the opportunity, and contains highlights of the substantive sections. It should concisely explain the current status of the company, its products and/or services, benefits to customers, and summary financial performance data. Where investment is being solicited, it should also include the amount of financing needed, and how investors will benefit and harvest their gains. With all this information, this summary should still be held to two pages, to insure its being read, and must generate enthusiasm about the proposal to entice the reader to consider the entire plan.

The closing summary, or "wrap-up," is a shorter summary, more directed to what is being asked of the reader. Supporting documentation includes relevant marketing research, and financial details and statements behind the financial proposal.

(2) Descriptive

In order to reasonably evaluate the business proposal, the reader needs some background on the proposed company, and the industry in which it will compete. A company mission statement can be an effective starting point in conveying the business concept. Also of interest are company goals, such as commitment to long-term results, innovation, productivity, and social responsibility.

Company information should also include the evolution of the business idea and the current stage of company development. The primary stakeholders and their roles should be discussed. Important accomplishments and milestones should be described.

Industry information should include the industry's size (such as total sales and profits), geographical dispersion, some history, and its current status. Competition should be discussed in terms of their offerings, market niches, and the extent of the threat to your proposed venture. There should be a discussion of the appropriateness of buying an existing business or acquiring a franchise. Quotes and statements from recent periodicals on the directions of the industry can be very useful. A projection of where the industry will be and your role in it over your planning horizon can be of considerable interest.

What are the significant factors affecting the market: cultural, attitudinal, demographic, legal, and technological? What are the trends in demand? What are the threats to the market?

The primary objective of this section is to convey your perception of the opportunity, and the relevance of the marketing research that convinced you that it is real and achievable. Of particular interest are the size of the market you will enter, your competitive advantage or unique strength, the company's "value adding" process, and market share expectations. These are the competitive issues in a strategic analysis, the full scope of which we will discuss later.

(3) Marketing

This section is essentially the marketing plan, which we discussed in Chapter 2. In this section, we need to clearly delineate our niche, and our distinctive competence. Investors are particularly interested in measuring the extent to which we are "market-driven;" the potential of the product's market, sales, and profit is more important than its appearance or technology.

We begin by describing our target market. What business are we in? What are we selling? How well positioned are we to provide it? Who are our customers (age, income, etc.)? How many of them are there? Is the number growing? The better and more accurate our source of these answers, the more compelling our proposal will be.

Our market research will often yield comments and statements from respected sources about buying patterns and trends; these can add strength to our statements. Where are our customers? How much do they buy? What are their motivators?

How well does our product meet their needs? From whom do they buy now? How are they best reached? How will we get our product to the customer? How will we advertise and promote it? Is the market seasonal?

Will we price our product as price leader, value leader, or prestige product? Is there any opportunity for a unique form of service or support? What market share can we reasonably expect? How long will it take us to get there?

Are there any barriers to entry: patents, sources of supply, distribution channels, etc.? How strong is brand loyalty? Can a small independent company compete? How are prices set? How important is the "experience curve?" Are there barriers to exit?

(4) Logistics

Location/Facilities

How much space do we need? How much equipment? What other facilities are important? Should we buy property and equipment or lease, which makes exit easier? How many employees do we need at startup? Is business location a significant factor? If so, what are our location criteria?

Location criteria can be applied at three levels: the city or metropolitan area; the neighborhood or section of town, and; a specific site. Is the city or section growing? How fast? Which parts? Is it strong in the demographics (age, income, etc.) critical to our success? Is it going "downhill?"

Specific sites within acceptable areas require a more detailed level of analysis. Is the area perceived as safe? How close are our competitors? How well are neighboring businesses doing? Is access easy? Parking available? Will there be zoning problems? Neighborhood resistance?

Legal Structure

The most common business structures are proprietorships, partnerships, and corporations. A proprietorship is simply a one-owner business. It is the most prevalent form (on the order of 70% of all businesses) because it is the simplest and least expensive to start.

A partnership is basically a proprietorship for multiple owners. Most are general partnerships, where each partner is held liable for the acts of the other partners. A limited partnership allows for general and limited partners; limited partners' liability is limited to their contributed capital.

The decision to enter a partnership should be based on whether or not you can "go it alone." The main reasons for people to feel they cannot are lack of money, skills, connections, and confidence. Are there other ways to address these needs?

If you chose to go into business with a partner, be sure to prepare a formal, written partnership agreement. This should address: the contribution each will make to the partnership, financial and personal; how business profits and losses will be apportioned; the salaries, and financial rights of each partner, and; provisions for changes in ownership, such as a sale, succession, or desire to bring in a new partner.

The corporation is a legal entity, separate from its owners. It is a more secure and better defined form for prospective lenders/investors. Incorporation is perceived as limiting the owner's liability, but personal guarantees are generally required whenever there is liability exposure.

The traditional form is called the C-Corporation. An S-Corporation is frequently preferable as a start-up form, since the losses expected in the early stages of the business may be applied to the owner's personal tax return. Other forms include: the LLC, or Limited Liability Corporation; Trusts, often for a specific time-frame or purpose, and; combinations of legal entities such as "Coops" and joint ventures.

The LLC is a common form used by startups, where taxable revenue "flows through" to the individual owners, but with corporate protections of personal assets. Often in the early stages of an LLC lenders will require that its owners sign a personal guarantee, which removes the corporate protection.

Enlist the legal and tax advice of the professionals as to which form suits your venture best.

Ownership Structure and Capitalization

Once the legal structure is decided upon, issues of distribution of ownership, and distribution of risks and benefits may be addressed. The primary decision to be made is whether the venture will be financed by the entrepreneur or whether there is a need for other stakeholders, and whether these stakeholders will be investors or lenders or some combination thereof.

The entrepreneur must keep the long-term in view. Shares of ownership may not seem very valuable at startup, but the entrepreneur could seriously regret having sold them so cheaply when the company prospers. On the other hand, borrowing for a new venture can be extremely difficult. The criteria for making decisions about capitalization are discussed at length in the financial section.

Human Resources

Many business plans are evaluated largely on the qualifications and commitment of the management team. The human resource plan must realistically assess the skills required for success of the venture, initially and over the long run, and match the skills and interests of the team to these requirements. Gaps must be filled with additional employees, learning activities, and/or consultants.

Once tasks are assigned, an effective responsibility structure must be designed. This structure would include the management of the organization, formal and informal advisors, and a board of directors. Methods of staying in touch with the market, such as association memberships and networking systems, can also be part of the human resource plan.

b. The Strategic Plan

(1) Purpose

The strategic plan defines the company's "competitive edge," that collection of factors that sets the business apart from its competitors and promotes its chances for success. It requires a clear evaluation of the competitive business climate and an intimate knowledge of the market for the entrepreneur's product. The strategic plan "borrows" from other sections of the business plan those items which help to establish the venture's uniqueness, and some overlap will be observed.

Small businesses are not scale models of big businesses; they are characterized by resource poverty and dependence on a fairly localized market. Their greater vulnerability to the consequences of a lack of focus stresses the importance of their strategic plan.

(2) Internal Factors

The foundation for the strategic plan is a clear mission statement for the venture. This statement can be developed by addressing the following questions:

What business am I in? The answer to this question is not as simple as it seems. A good example of an industry group that failed to take a broader view is the railroads. If they had viewed their business as transportation rather than *trains-and-tracks,* then there would be airlines named *Union Pacific* and *Illinois Central.*

Other questions useful to mission development include: Whom is our product intended to satisfy? What customer needs are being satisfied? How are these needs being satisfied, that is, by which of our methods or products?

Other issues relevant to our internal analysis include identification of our corporate philosophy. Examples would be our commitment to employee fulfillment, quality management, partnership with customers and suppliers, and good corporate citizenship.

A primary company goal is frequently to maximize long-term stakeholder wealth. Secondary goals might include targets for market share, innovation, productivity, physical and financial resources, manager performance and development, worker performance and attitude, job satisfaction, and social responsibility.

An important strategic option is in how we price our product (as a price leader, value leader, or prestige product). Other options include the way in which we differentiate ourselves from the competition, and the particular subset of the market, or niche, we seek to serve.

Case Study 6-1   Tammany Supply, Inc. (C)

INTRODUCTION

Tammany Supply, Inc. (TSI), a plumbing supply distributor in Covington, LA, got off to a running start in mid-1998 (see the "B" case). The Vinturella family had tested whether the market was large enough to support a supply house by opening a branch of Southland Plumbing Supply, Inc. there in early 1997. John Vinturella, oldest member of the company's second generation, started up the branch, then negotiated a buyout with the rest of the family to operate it as a separate company, TSI. John became sole owner of TSI, and gave up his stake in Southland.

TSI exceeded $1million in sales in its first full year, 1999, $2 million in 2003, and $3 million the very next year. Pre-tax profits during this period approached $100,000 per year (see Figure 6-1).

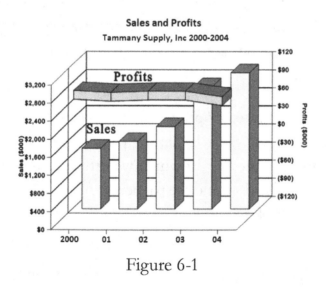

Figure 6-1

TSI's timing was fortuitous, opening just as its market area, western St. Tammany parish, was becoming the New Orleans suburb of choice for upscale professionals. TSI's marketing approach, unconventional by supply house standards, contributed to this success; they openly courted retail sales, even advertising on television. By the time other supply houses began to look covetously at the market, TSI was firmly established. Their pre-emptive strike, opening before the opportunity was obvious, had created a barrier to others' entry.

THE "CRASH"

A more serious barrier to entry arose in 2005. The collapse of world oil prices took a devastating toll on the Louisiana economy, and the high-end suburb of the state's largest metropolitan area was particularly hard-hit. While TSI showed only a slight sales decrease in 2005, and a profit increase, the bottom fell out the next year. Sales fell almost 40% in 2006, and even lower in 2007.

TSI showed a profit on operations in 2006, barely half that of the year before, but did not charge off any of its looming credit losses. The homebuilding industry runs largely on credit, and depends on a steady or growing demand. When that demand falls off, builders are left with unsold houses and huge interest payments; contractors do not get paid, and cannot pay for their materials. TSI paid for its goods before it sold them, so it had no one to help it share the pain. When most of TSI's bad-debt losses were written off in 2007, the operating loss for the year exceeded $100,000 (see Figure 6-2).

Figure 6-2

It was obvious that changes in the external environment had caused a need for reevaluating TSI's strategy, and the sense of free-fall to the company's fortunes made this need seem immediate.

WHAT DO WE DO NOW?

The options available to TSI were limited by the size of their market, the condition of the local economy, and their resource position. Inventory had shot up in 2004, in response to the higher level of business, and the increased sales raised accounts receivable accordingly. By 2005, the slowdown was becoming apparent, and TSI was beginning to get its inventory down, while stepping up collections to improve its cash position (see Figure 6-3).

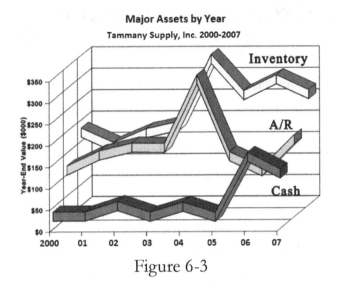

Figure 6-3

Cash was sufficient at the end of 2007, $70,000 or so above usual levels, to support some diversification. This could take the form of additional inventory items, or the startup of some new operation. Related businesses were considered for the vacant spaces in TSI's building created by the collapse of appliance and ceiling fan stores. But could TSI succeed where so many homebuilding dependent businesses in the area were failing? Were their chances any better in a field unrelated to construction?

In any case, TSI's core business had shrunk by 40%. Expenses could be cut some, but to cut them enough to matter would have left the company considerably less than a full-service supply house, and much more vulnerable to competition. John was also reluctant to cut TSI's excellent work force, even though they were working well below capacity.

Adding to John's problems with keeping TSI viable was the problem of meeting mortgage payments on a building that was now barely half occupied. Replacement tenants were nowhere to be found, and TSI could hardly bear to absorb the rental shortfall.

TSI's options were few, and decidedly unattractive. They could return the building to the bank and negotiate a lower monthly payment as a renter. They could downsize their payroll to a level appropriate to sales volume. Or, they could try to apply the vacant space and underutilized human resources to generate some added sales volume and profits; the challenge lay in deciding how.

STUDY QUESTIONS

1. Did decisions made during the good times contribute to the difficulty of dealing with the crash? Could the assets have been managed better? Could adjustments have been made more smoothly?
2. Should the bad times ahead have been foreseen by TSI management? Were they slow to respond? Were their actions appropriate? Effective?
3. Why is John so reluctant to scale the business down to a level appropriate to sales? What would the longer-term consequences be? How would the competition view such a move? What would it do to the chances for recovery as the economy improves?
4. What are TSI's strategic options? What information would you gather to help evaluate possible new product

lines or related ventures? What new offerings would fit well with traditional plumbing supply lines? Is it better to sell more things to existing customers, or bring in new customers?

5. If new lines are added, is it better to re-train existing personnel or replace some with new employees experienced in the new line? If the re-train option is chosen, how long might it be before TSI can effectively market the new products?

6. How effectively can TSI broaden its offerings with $70,000 in cash? Would it be better to preserve the cash to ride out the difficult period? Is this any time for "adventurism," or should John concentrate on holding on to what is left of his core business?

7. How does John's ownership of the building, outside of TSI, affect his options? Is he caught in any conflict of objectives? Would he act differently on behalf of TSI if the building were owned by someone else? Should he try to sell the building?

8. Is now the time to sell the business? Are the regional chains likely to still be interested? How fast can the business be "turned around?" What would you do?

(3) External/Competitive Environment

Once we have set internal objectives, we must examine the external and competitive environments in which we will be trying to achieve them.

The external environment consists of those factors which are largely outside our control, but affect the market for our product. Examples of these factors include general economic conditions, regulations, technological developments, and consumer demographics and attitudes. This environment is very dynamic, but some attempt must be made at projecting its changes.

Analysis of the competitive environment must begin with consideration of whether there are any barriers to the entry of a new competitor into the market. How strong is consumer loyalty to existing brands? How important are economies of scale; can a small independent firm compete? Are capital requirements prohibitive? Is there some proprietary technology that puts prospective entrants in a serious competitive disadvantage? Is access to raw materials or to distribution channels limited in some way? Are new entrants limited by permit restrictions or regulations?

The competitive structure of the industry is another important consideration. Are there a few dominant firms, or is the industry fairly fragmented? Will current competitors attempt to "punish" new entrants, such as through a price war, heavy advertising, or exercising their clout with key suppliers? Is there some geographic niche we can serve? What factors create cost advantages or disadvantages? How important is a firm's position on the learning and experience curves? How are prices set? Is demand rising, even, or falling? Are there exit barriers that raise the risk of entry?

Relative strengths of our strategic partners must also be considered. What is the bargaining power of suppliers? How wide is our choice of suppliers? Is it costly for us to switch? Can our suppliers compete with us for the same customers? How important is our industry to our suppliers?

Do buyers have a wide choice of vendors? Can they make our product themselves? Are there less expensive or superior substitutes to our product in some segments of the market?

(4) SWOT (Strengths/Weaknesses/Opportunities/Threats) Analysis

The major strength of a company is that which most clearly distinguishes it from the competition, referred to as its "distinctive competence." It can take many forms, but it must be identified and built upon. This competitive advantage can be in a primary aspect of the business (manufacture, sales, service), or a secondary one (support, personnel, purchasing, etc.). It is the critical factor in the company's value-adding process.

While the venture's weaknesses need not be emphasized, they should be recognized and identified. A plan to overcome them, or at least minimize their impact, is far more credible than denying that they exist.

Certainly, the opportunity addressed initially is central to the business plan, but a discussion of peripheral and/or future opportunities demonstrates a deeper understanding of the full range of possibilities of the venture. These can include a broader geographic area, wider product line, and new applications for current products.

Just as weaknesses must be recognized, so must threats to the future success of the business. These can be internal, such as a concept which can be easily copied, or limitations of working capital. Threats can also be external, such as an economic downturn, shifting demographics, or technological developments. Competitive factors can also come into play, such as entry of a major company in a related business.

c. Elements of Style

Now that we have all the components of the business plan laid out, we can begin to craft the final product. Some "first impressions" criteria for a good business plan are that it be attractive and interesting, well organized and carefully edited, and easy to understand.

Readers must be led through our analysis in a way that leads them to accept our conclusions. Our primary objective is to convey that there is an opportunity, that we are equipped to seize it, and that "the numbers work." It is helpful to be concise and focused, and to avoid vague and/or unsubstantiated claims. Potential problems must be anticipated and addressed, leading to a convincing likelihood of success. Projections must be rigorously realistic and objective, and based on reasonable assumptions.

M. John Storey, principal of Storey Communications, suggests that we: "Keep the plan incredibly simple. Talk in pictures. Back up your images with a phone-book-size financial package, but only at the end. Never allow a reader to say 'Too complicated, not for me,' on the first page." He also cautions that we "leave out the mumbo-jumbo," keeping the focus on "who's going to buy what product, and at what price?" He urges the use of summaries to help plant the key facts in a prospective investor's mind: profit, potential, costs, key customers.

Katie Muldoon, president of Muldoon & Baer, suggests that the plan, which she views as a prospectus, should reflect your personality and ambitions: "Investors bet on people, and the prospectus is an opportunity to sell your qualities. Make sure the writing reflects your drive and professionalism." She adds that "It's like any other selling job. You've got to know your audience, write to your audience."

"Deal killers" can include: carelessness in preparation (what does this convey?); insufficient belief in the project by its principals, and; a lack of comfort with and confidence in the company principals on the part of prospective stakeholders. More often, business proposals fail for more tangible reasons, such as: success depending on too many or too shaky contingencies; an inadequate return to justify the risks, and; the absence of a "graceful way out," that is a credible exit strategy, for stakeholders.

Where we are seeking financial stakeholders, we would like to get the opportunity to present the highlights of our proposition in person. While a request for an oral presentation could be met with resistance, A. David Silver of ADS Financial Services suggests that "lenders and investors are more interested in tenacious entrepreneurs than in relaxed or casual" ones. He cautions, though, that you "balance your persistence, so that you don't appear 'pushy'."

Oral presentations are generally characterized by a very short time allowance, and a somewhat skeptical audience. Make your case quickly; Storey suggests that you should be able to explain the business opportunity in 25 words or less, leading them to suggest "tell me more." Tell the prospect what's in it for them, particularly what benefits they will enjoy if they invest.

The oral presentation must answer many of the same questions as the written; it can be more difficult due to time constraints, or easier because we have more senses to appeal to. Computer presentation packages can be used to generate attractive, professional visual aids. Do not use copies of spreadsheets or printed pages as visuals; design "pithy" slides that are not too "busy." Use the visuals as an outline of your talk so that you do not have to refer to notes. Be sure to adapt your presentation to the medium, and to your audience.

Rehearse your presentation until you are very comfortable with it. Present it to a knowledgeable and objective friend for feedback. Time it to make sure you do not overstay your welcome.

Corporate trainer and speaker Lani Arredondo suggests the AMMA rule for presentations, that they be: attention-getting;

meaningful; memorable, and; activating. She stresses that the purpose of a presentation is to persuade. She cautions that: perception is more powerful than fact; people are inundated with data, and; people forget fast. A presentation must be balanced between information elements and relational ones, those that relate to your audience. Ideally, the presentation should lead directly into the prospect asking how they can participate.

Summary

We can evaluate our business plan according to the following checklist:

(1) General

Is it clear what business the company is in? Is the concept well thought out? Expressed effectively?

Is the overall presentation concise, businesslike? Is the plan attractive? Well-written? Interesting?

Does the plan "sell?" Generate enthusiasm?

(2) Marketing Plan

How good is the market research? How applicable is it to this specific business? How well do the principals understand the industry? Is the target market clearly identified? Is it the right market? Is it big enough? Is it growing? Is the marketing approach credible and convincing?

(3) Strategic Issues

Is the business sufficiently differentiated? Is its competitive advantage clear and convincing? Is product positioning and pricing appropriate to the competitive situation?

Are company strengths sufficient for success? Are any company weaknesses fatal? Are all promising opportunities recognized? Are all significant threats adequately considered?

Are the human resources indicated sufficient to the task? Used well? Is the scope of operations appropriate to the opportunities? Are the keys to success clearly identified?

(4) Overall

Is the plan convincing? Are the principals realistic about where the industry is headed and the competitive situation, and reasonable in their projections? Are they capable of implementing the plan?

Review Questions

1. What is the major purpose of a business plan? Is a business plan needed where the entrepreneur can finance the venture without assistance?
2. What are the primary components of the business plan? Is there a standard format? An appropriate length? A specific audience for whom it is written?
3. What are the major objectives of the marketing plan?
4. What are the logistical issues that should be resolved in the plan?

5. What is the purpose of the strategic plan?

6. Does the form and quality of the business plan affect our chance of convincing prospective stakeholders? Aren't most investors and lenders too sophisticated to be swayed by form? How do they use the plan to evaluate us?

Case Study 6-2	Tammany Supply, Inc. (D)

INTRODUCTION

From its 1998 startup through 2005, Tammany Supply, Inc. (TSI) of Covington, LA was the dominant plumbing supply wholesaler in western St. Tammany parish. St. Tammany, an upscale suburb of New Orleans, was one of the country's fastest growing counties during this period, and TSI's growth rate reflected it.

Sales evened off in 2005, then fell precipitously in 2006 as the collapse of world oil prices took the energy out of the Louisiana economy. Sales fell even further in 2007 as TSI suffered its first money-losing year (see the "C" case).

New residential construction, which had been a mainstay for TSI, fell off dramatically as homes were left vacant all over the parish by people leaving Louisiana to find work. TSI had to perform a re-evaluation of their strategy, and do it fast, to cope with a 40% decrease in their core business.

DIVERSIFICATION

As the "crash" damages to TSI were being assessed, its president, John Vinturella, began to write the company's first formal business plan. This plan consisted primarily of a strategic analysis and an implementation plan to get TSI back to profitability. The 2007-09 plan served as a road map for the way back, with some mid-course corrections made in a 2008 update; the 2010-12 plan was a bit more comprehensive, since the air of crisis had been removed. The 2011 update serves to illustrate that planning is not just for startups, but is an ongoing process.

The following excerpt from the plan describes the recovery strategy:

> "The decreased demand was addressed on three fronts: the impact on sales volume was softened by diversifying product lines, cash was preserved by a gradual selling off of inventory, and expenses were cut.

Diversification of product lines was intended to increase retail sales, particularly in remodeling and add-on items. To that end the company began emphasizing spas and whirlpools, and became a master distributor for *Toro* sprinkler systems. In 2007 TSI opened the *Outdoor Living Center* (OLC), a retailer of outdoor and patio furniture and accessories. In 2008 the company opened a franchise of *Singer Kitchens and Baths* (SKB), strengthening its cabinet sales effort and adding appliances. In 2009 the company broadened its water treatment and air-conditioning supply offerings.

Less glamorous, but just as vital were the inventory reduction and cost-cutting campaigns. Low turnover items were returned to the manufacturer or offered to other suppliers and the public at break-even pricing or less. Staff was reduced by attrition, one truck was retired, insurance was tightened, and some functions previously contracted out were brought back in."

By the 2011 update, a preliminary report on results could be made:

"The last three years have seen the end of "free-fall," as business stabilized but did not really improve. Sales volume is recovering, but margins have remained weak; 2008 was a moderately good year, 2009 a moderately bad one, and 2010 was essentially break-even."

Note: Minor discrepancies may be noted between the financial data in the business plan, and that reported in this series of cases. Data in the plan is based on statements generated by TSI, whereas data in the cases is based on tax returns, and reflects accounting adjustments that improve accuracy. None of the differences are large enough to affect the discussions of strategy.

Some mid-course correction was called for:

"At the end of 2010, by mutual agreement, TSI returned control of the SKB store to the franchiser. SKB continues to operate the store, effectively shutting TSI out of the cabinet business.

Despite our high hopes for the kitchen business, it did not create as good a fit with our overall operation as we had hoped, and the attractive margins were eaten up by heavy personnel demands.

The result of this decision is a slight downsizing of our operation.... In 2010, SKB sales represented almost 15% of TSI sales."

Some good news could be found:

"On the positive side, we feel that we can make up this volume in our mainstream business. We see a definite increase in construction activity, and our two local competitors left the area in October 2010."

The local competitors referred to were Park Supply, a Picayune MS company which opened a Covington branch in 2006, and Plumbing Specialty of New Orleans which entered the market in 2008. All was not quiet on the competitive front, however; Southern Pipe, a regional chain based in Meridian MS, announced in early 2011 that they would open a western St. Tammany branch by the end of the year.

Since TSI could hardly survive another year like 2007, the following three years were projected to be the recovery period. It was a spotty recovery at best. Sales drifted upward, exceeding $2 million again by 2010. Of the three, only 2008 was profitable, and would not have been but for a large income tax refund reflecting the huge loss of the previous year (see Figure 6-4).

Still, some cause for optimism could be found:

"We hope that the worst is behind us. All reasonably questionable debts are written off and expenses are tightly controlled. State and area economic outlook have improved, and the local recovery seems to have some strength."

Projections for 2011-12 show an expectation of a return to profitability on the order of $30,000 per year.

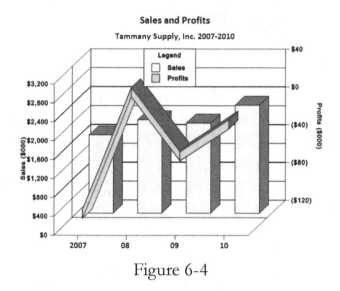

Figure 6-4

STUDY QUESTIONS

1. Was 2007 too late for TSI to write its first business plan? Would a formal written strategic plan in 2005 have helped guide the company through the difficult period? Could it have helped soften the impact? What was the purpose of the 2010 plan?

2. Evaluate the strategic plan. Does the assessment of external forces seem reasonable? Are internal capabilities reasonably assessed? Does the strategy selection follow logically from the assessments?

3. Are the goals expressed too modest, reasonable, or too ambitious? Are they relevant to the problems facing TSI? Are the tools necessary to their accomplishment identified?

4. Is management in control and on target? Are they collecting the right information, and evaluating it properly, as a guide to future actions?

5. How successful has the diversification strategy been? Should it be abandoned, or simply refined? Do the reasons for dropping SKB make sense? How is SKB significantly different from the other forms of diversification?

6. Why did two competitors move in after the crash? Why do you think they could not make it? Why were the earlier entries small independents, while the regional chain waited until an apparent recovery was under way? What effect do you expect the 2011 entry of a competitor with "deep pockets" will have on TSI's recovery?

7. Are you confident about TSI's prospects for the remaining two years of this planning period? What would you do differently?

STEP 7

Fund the Venture

Chapter Objectives:

On completing this chapter, you should be able to:

- Forecast sales for your business
- Prepare pro forma statements
- Estimate capital requirements
- Pursue funding to start your business

The Financial Plan

(1) Forecasting

The sales forecast "scales" the business. It determines the amount of people, space and equipment the venture will require which in turn can be related to financial requirements. While forecasting is an uncomfortable process for most people, an orderly approach can make it seem less like guesswork.

Unit sales and expected selling price can be estimated and extended to yield sales dollars. Comparative information adds credibility and perspective; government and trade association websites and publications can be productive sources.

Key questions to ask ourselves are: How big is the market? Is it growing? What share can we reasonably expect? How long will it take us to get there? Often, separate statements are produced for optimistic, expected, and pessimistic (OEP) projections.

Industry norms for gross margin can be adapted to our concept to yield gross margin dollars. We must then estimate our cost structure. The following section discusses how this might be done. Again, industry norms modified by our experience and concept of operation can be very useful.

At this point, a break-even analysis (see Chapter 4) can be performed. Fixed costs, or those which are independent of our sales level, should be separated from variable costs for the analysis.

Does the market potential support the break-even sales level? Where does this sales level fall within our OEP spectrum? Should we proceed if break-even requires our most optimistic sales projection? Should we re-examine our numbers? Which can be changed or improved (sales, margins, expenses)? Should we suffer some margin to increase sales? Can expenses be cut?

(2) The Pro Forma Income Statement

In the early stages of the business, sales are growing rapidly (we hope!) from zero to some expected level over several months; initial marketing efforts may take 6 months to dent the public awareness. For a pre-startup income statement to accurately represent this high state of flux, it is recommended that it show performance by month for the first three years, or until profitability is achieved.

The income section of the statement shows the sales estimate and cost of goods sold (CGS), and the difference - generally referred to as gross margin dollars, or margin. CGS is generally expressed as a percentage of sales. Margin dollars are then available to pay expenses, with the remainder being the before-tax profit. See *Tammany Supply Case A* for an example of this process.

Categories for the expense section of the statement can be grouped into: personnel; administrative; sales expense, and; operations. Methods of allocation between these groups can vary widely, but this structure is useful for considering the form our expenses will take.

Personnel expenses consist of salaries (often split into "Officers" and "Others") and related costs, such as payroll taxes and benefits.

Administrative costs can include accounting and legal expenses, bad debt and collection costs, bank charges, depreciation, and interest. Estimation of interest paid is iterative, that is, the amount to be borrowed must be estimated, yielding a number for interest expense; this is part of the profit/loss picture, which determines how much must be borrowed. Seldom are more than 2 or 3 passes required to converge to a final estimate, and spreadsheet programs make the process simple.

Sales expenses include advertising and promotion, and sales commissions. Operations costs are such things as rent, vehicle expense, utilities, and supplies.

For the purposes of estimation, it is best to use the detailed categories to come up with numbers that we can "sink our teeth into." These can then be consolidated into the above groupings when the business enters more of a "steady-state."

In building a spreadsheet *pro forma* income statement, we are building a "model" of the business. It should be constructed using relationships rather than constant values, such as margin and some expense categories as a percent of sales, sales increases with time as a percentage growth, etc. Then we can experiment with a range of reasonable alternatives for our "control variables," such as estimated sales, and profit margins.

(3) The Pro Forma Balance Sheet

Whereas the income statement describes company performance over some period of time, such as a month or year, the balance sheet shows the value of the company at a point in time (opening day, end of the fiscal year). This value is expressed as the value of the company's assets, and its liabilities, with the difference being net worth or owners' equity.

Assets are classified as "Current" or "Other." Current assets include cash and "liquid" investments such as certificates of deposit, and items (relatively) readily converted to cash, such as inventory and accounts receivable. Often the values presented account for a portion of inventory being obsolete, and a portion of accounts receivable being uncollectible, but this is not applicable to startup ventures. Other assets are primarily fixed that is, have some relatively long service life over which their value is amortized. These include property and improvements, vehicles, and equipment. Depreciation schedules are generally "aggressive," taking maximum advantage of tax law, and frequently cause fixed asset values to be understated.

Liabilities are generally classified as "Current" and "Long-Term." Current liabilities consist of items due in the relatively short term, such as accruals of sales and payroll taxes, and "Accounts Payable," or invoices for goods received. Long-term liabilities are generally "Notes Payable" with fixed repayment terms.

The difference between assets and liabilities, as though the company were being liquidated, is the net worth of the business, or "Owners' Equity." The balance sheet must be consistent with the income statement. Accumulated profits become gain in equity, purchases become assets, note payments decrease loan balances, depreciation reduces asset values.

See *Tammany Supply Case B* for an example of a summary Balance Sheet.

(4) Capital Requirements

The capital requirements of the business can be developed as the sum of: pre-startup outlay; fixed assets needed within the startup period, and; accumulated operating losses until break-even or better is achieved. The requirement is generally met by some combination of cash and loans; we will discuss sources of funds in the next section.

Determination of the capital required for a successful startup is an iterative process, greatly simplified by spreadsheet programs. Appended to the bottom of the income statement spreadsheet can be a cash flow section, showing cash in, plus profit or less loss, is equal to cash out. Actually two adjustments are required to this nominal equation: depreciation must be added back in, because it is a non-cash expense, and; the principal portion of a note payment must be subtracted, because it does not affect expenses but does "transform" cash into equity.

What is needed in the pre-startup period? Generally there are fixed assets required, primarily the property from which we will operate or the cost of modifying leased property for our purposes, with the next largest commitment being equipment. We must open with an appropriate level of inventory. There are probably some salary, supplies, and other expenses associated with setting up to open.

Some of these are "sunk" costs, that is, unrecoverable even if we shut the business down. Others can be recovered only at "fire-sale" rates on shutdown. These losses may be considered exit costs, and may be thought of as the minimum loss should the venture not "get off the ground."

Other fixed assets may be needed after opening for business, but before profitability is reached. To the extent that we can delay their acquisition without harming our business prospects, we can lessen our capital requirements. Often we can lease equipment, sometimes with credit towards later purchase, until our longer-term needs become clearer.

Pre-startup outlays and equipment needs are fairly tangible and easy to conceptualize, but the other component of our capital requirements needs is more difficult to estimate. The amount of our accumulated operating losses depends on sales and expense estimates reaching well into the future.

One way to estimate accumulated operating losses (AOL) is to run our model with a zero starting cash amount, and scan month-ending cash until this balance reaches its most negative, that is before profitability begins to turn the balance back upward. This most negative value is our best estimate of AOL, and our starting cash must be this amount plus some contingency "cushion."

We now have all the components of our capital requirement, and it is important that we not "cut it too close." Some conservatism must be applied to the model, and some contingencies allowed for. We want to provide enough to make the business a long-term success; potentially profitable businesses often close because of being "starved" for operating capital in the startup period.

It is also important to document the assumptions made in arriving at our estimates, and to establish milestones and landmarks for our financial performance to "calibrate" it against expectations; it is much harder to be objective about how we are doing once into the venture and possibly even faced with whether it is worth the effort to continue. Where there are investors or lenders involved, part of their financial commitment to the venture may be contingent on reaching these milestones.

Once capital requirements are established, we must consider whether we can fund the startup ourselves. Otherwise, we now enter the fundraising stage.

(5) Crowdfunding

Crowdfunding is defined by Investopedia (http://www.investopedia.com/terms/c/crowdfunding.asp) as the use of small amounts of capital from a large number of individuals to finance a new business venture.

Crowdfunding makes use of the easy accessibility of vast networks of friends, family and colleagues through social media websites like Facebook, Twitter and LinkedIn to get the word out about a new business and attract investors. Crowdfunding has the potential to increase entrepreneurship by expanding the pool of investors from whom funds can be raised beyond the traditional circle of owners, relatives and venture capitalists.

This form of raising funds was made possible by the JOBS Act (2012) which removed an earlier prohibition on general solicitation or general advertising for securities offerings. There are limitations on how much can be raised through such solicitations. For a summary of these limitations, see http://www.forbes.com/sites/chancebarnett/2015/03/26/infographic-sec-democratizes-equity-crowdfunding-with-jobs-act-title-iv/

Crowdfunding is an excellent way for start-ups to obtain the financing and exposure they need so they can verify, execute, and enhance growth.

The approach is simple enough: You decide on a suitable website according to your campaign theme and purpose. Once a platform is determined, you contact the public by sharing your venture's powerful message, usually in a video that passionately explains the essentials of your project, and establish attractive rewards for potential financiers. You set a target amount you wish to reach at the end of a specific time (normally about 40 days) and backers can select how much they want to commit. Generally, it's free to sign up for a campaign.

Some platforms allow you to collect money only when your target is reached, so you can only access the funds if you reach 100 percent or more of your funding objective. You collect nothing if the crowd does not donate the figure you seek. There is no penalty for not attaining your target; the funds are simply returned to individual contributors. Other platforms provide you with the funds whether the crowd reached the target or not. Only the campaign period matters. For successful projects, the platforms take an average commission of five percent of the funds raised. They take nothing when the target is not attained.

There is a crowdfunding site for every business niche. See https://www.wrike.com/blog/26-top-crowdfunding-sites-by-niche/

Kickstarter.com The most well-known of the crowdfunding websites, Kickstarter focuses on creative endeavors including design, the arts (film, publishing, music), gaming and technology. While Kickstarter can't be used to fund businesses per se, it does accept products and has had some remarkably successful campaigns, including about 50 that have generated over a million dollars in funding. Kickstarter "curates" its projects, meaning it has a rigorous submission process, and if you aren't approved to post, it can be quite disappointing.

Indiegogo.com Originally launched with a focus on film, Indiegogo pivoted to include funding for literally anything and is becoming known for financing personal and cause-related campaigns such as that for the bullied bus monitor, which raised over $700,000. It accepts all projects without review. As Indiegogo says on its website, "Our platform is available to anyone, anywhere, to raise money for anything." While its success fee at 4 percent is 1 percent lower than most websites (which charge 5 percent), it does charge one of the highest fees in the industry -- 9 percent -- if you don't meet your goal.

The benefits of crowdfunding include the following:

- **Access to capital.** In many instances, you may not even have to give up equity. Some funding may simply be donations. Other investors may just require early access to the product you are developing.
- **Risk reduction.** There are no loans to repay, no collateral to pledge.
- **Marketing advantages.** The public is made aware of your product early in the process. Even those who do not invest become potential customers.

There is another category of crowdfunding, often referred to as equity crowdfunding. This form of funding allows *accredited* investors to share in the expected financial return of the business. To be accredited, an investor must meet standards set by the US Securities and Exchange Commission (SEC) as to income and net worth. These standards are outlined in http://www.sec.gov/answers/accred.htm.

(6) Other Sources of Funds

While the discussion of capital requirements may have seemed pessimistic, with its mention of exit costs and deciding when to "pull the plug," pessimism is what the entrepreneur at fundraising will be greeted with. It is the entrepreneur's dream, about which he or she has great difficulty being objective, being presented to skeptical prospective stakeholders, that is investors and lenders. They have seen several ventures fail, but never have they seen an entrepreneur who allowed for that possibility in advance. What would it say to them if that possibility were acknowledged?

Prospective investors generally expect a substantial financial commitment to the venture by the entrepreneur. Their sense is that it should not be easy for the entrepreneur to give the venture a half-hearted try, leaving the consequences of failure to the stakeholders. The entrepreneur's financial commitment (EFC) is often a combination of personal funds and investments and loans from "friendly" sources, that is family and friends.

Assuming then an EFC of 50%, what are our options for raising the other half of our capital requirement? The basic decision to be made is how much will be raised by selling equity, that is shares of ownership in the venture, and how much will be borrowed.

To the entrepreneur, the advantage of using **equity financing** is that *the investor is sharing the risks of the venture*, and that this lowers expenses since there is no debt service to be paid. The investor also shares the rewards, however, and the entrepreneur must be careful not to sell the equity too cheaply.

What do we have to offer prospective investors? For most, their primary interest is in a high return on their investment, through dividends and appreciation. Other considerations might be opportunities for tax benefits, and for director and consulting income. Of generally lesser interest are non-cash rewards, such as privileged information, access to new products, and "psychic income." There is little appeal to most investors in being a long-term minority owner in a closely-held business, so some way of "cashing out," such as a provision for company buy-back, must be offered.

How do we identify prospective investors? We could sell stock to the public. The Initial Public Offering (IPO) is seldom an option for startups, however, unless they have a high growth potential proprietary product. The high costs involved make about $2 million the minimum feasible IPO; more often they are in the $8-15 million range. According to *Going Public: The IPO Reporter*, there were 275 IPO's in 2014, raising $85.2 billion.

What about the venture capital market? Venture capitalists look for generally larger deals and impressive returns. Many fund projects only in specific industries; some work only from referrals from within their "network." Carol Steinberg, in *"Success Selling,"* puts the odds of receiving venture capital funding in perspective: "Each year a venture capitalist fields

400 to 500 deals, seriously reviews 40 or 50, and funds only 4 or 5."

Less visible as a source of startup capital are individual investors, known as "angels," who typically invest $20,000 to a few million dollars in private companies. While we must generally "recruit" such investors ourselves, angels are thought to represent a pool of risk capital in excess of $20 billion each year.

While stakeholders are hard to find at startup, sources of assistance are available. A good starting point is the U.S. Small Business Administration (SBA). The SBA's primary lending program -- the 7(a) Loan Program -- guarantees as much as 85 percent of loans up to $150,000 and 75 percent of loans of more than $150,000. The maximum loan amount is $5 million.

Debt financing, on the other hand, *adds to our fixed costs, but makes no claim beyond the amount of the debt* no matter how great our success. Standards for debt financing are generally very difficult for startups to meet; lenders are not generally willing to share the risk with you. If you are turned down by a lender, ask them for specific reasons. If the reasons cannot be countered with this lender, the insight gained can be used to strengthen the presentation to the next.

A credit line, which we draw upon only as needed, can be used to hold down interest costs. Easy payment terms from suppliers of startup inventory can lower borrowing requirements. Assets of the business can be used as collateral, but a personal guarantee will almost always be required. This commits your personal assets to repayment of the loan.

(7) Finance Plan

Is startup capitalization adequate? Is it used well? Are all startup costs recognized? Are sales and sales growth expectations realistic?

Are sales projections credible? Achievable? Are expense estimates reasonable? Complete? Are margin goals realistic? Convincing? Is there a solid basis for estimates (industry norms, experience), or do they appear to be guesswork? Is the progression of income/expense estimates credible?

Are income, cash flow, and balance statements consistent? Is cash well managed? Is the cash management strategy clear? Does the total package (text, statements, assumptions, etc.) present a clear and complete picture of the financial position?

(8) Presentations

1. Are you well-rehearsed and comfortable with the content? Does your delivery convey professionalism and enthusiasm?
2. Is the presentation clear and concise? Does it stress benefits to the prospect? Is it attractive and interesting? Does it end with a call to action?
3. What is the basis of the financial plan? How can we forecast sales? How can we test projections for reasonability?

4. How do we determine the capital requirements of a venture? What are typical startup investments?

5. What are the primary sources of funds for startup businesses? What percentage, on average, comes from personal resources?

6. What are the two primary types of venture financing? What are the relative merits of each?

7. What are our options for equity financing? How are our chances?

8. How are our chances for commercial loans? How can we reduce our borrowing requirements?

9. Is an oral presentation to prospects necessary? How desirable is it? What are the keys to an effective oral presentation?

STEP 8

Grow the Business

Chapter Objectives:

On completing this chapter, you should be able to:

- Discuss and understand the stages in the development of a business
- Apply the principles of cash flow management and financial ratio analysis to the management of the small business
- Consider the rapid-growth strategy for a successful business, including the demands placed on its owner, and consideration of international opportunities.
- Identify owner "disengagement," and evaluate selling the business as an option

a. Beyond Startup

In a classic *Harvard Business Review* article, Neil Churchill and Virginia Lewis identify and describe what they refer to as "The five stages of small business growth."

Until now, we have focused primarily on Stage 1, or what they term as "**Existence**." This stage is characterized by acquiring customers and delivering satisfactory products and/or services in sufficient quantity to become a viable business.

Stage 2, after having demonstrated some market acceptance, may be considered "**Survival**." In this stage, we may consider our primary challenge to be generating enough cash flow to stay in business and financing growth to achieve an economic return on our capital and efforts. We will discuss cash flow and progress measurement in the following section.

Stage 3 is when we may consider ourselves a "**Success**." Success is actually less a stage than a plateau; it also represents a significant crossroads. Many business owners use this plateau as a launching pad for growth, passing through a Stage 4: **"Take-Off"** to Stage 5: **"Resource Maturity."** We will discuss the growth path in a later section.

Other successful business owners choose to enjoy life on the plateau. Churchill and Lewis refer to this as "**Disengagement**," characterized by the owner passing responsibilities on to professional staff members. The business then generally takes on a defensive posture, focusing more on holding its position rather than exploring any new frontiers. We will discuss disengagement in the final section of this chapter.

Before proceeding to the stages after "existence," however, we will briefly discuss one of the cornerstones of building and maintaining a successful business, namely a commitment to ethical behavior, community involvement, and social responsibility. Usually, the first tests of our business ethics occur while working for others; these tests become more difficult as we consider, and then pursue entrepreneurial opportunities.

(1) The Ethical Individual

It should go without saying that the ethical individual does not steal from or lie to an employer or a customer; these are the easy situations in which to determine ethical behavior. But what about all the little opportunities to shade the truth, or leave out an important detail, or make unauthorized use of company resources, or pad an expense account; where does salesmanship or discretion end, and unethical behavior begin?

The person working for someone else while considering starting a new venture can also encounter some difficult ethical dilemmas. How long can the prospective entrepreneur work for a firm while planning to start up a competitor? What actions within that role are permissible, and which could be considered advancing their personal cause at their firm's expense?

For the startup entrepreneur, the temptations are great to over-represent assets and understate liabilities. Most are strapped for resources, and fear the unvarnished truth may not be sufficient to get the needed resource commitments.

(2) The Ethical Company

Businesses operate with the presumption of trustworthiness. Those that violate that trust soon run out of one-time victims. Long-term success is built on lasting relationships, which depend on kept promises and fair treatment.

It is not a wishful or idealistic observation to say that a company does well by doing good. Highly ethical companies earn the trust of their customers and other strategic partners, and this leads to mutually beneficial relationships. Employees are proud to work for companies that treat them with respect, and their performance reflects it.

But there is more to ethical behavior than honesty and consideration. A broader term that reflects a proactive component is social responsibility. Companies that invest in their communities are rewarded many times over. Internships and summer jobs for local students, sponsorship of community organizations, and participation in food banks and charity drives are all ways to strengthen our bonds to the community while giving us a justifiably great feeling about our company.

Little good comes to us that is not a return on some investment we have made. There are few professional rewards as great as the feeling of being a contributing member of the community, and of the extended family that we and our associates can become.

Minicase 8-1:	How could that be an ethical problem?

Sherry Blaylock was ahead of her time when she started *Net Profits, Inc.*, a consulting firm for businesses considering an Internet presence, but it is beginning to pay off in the spring of 1996. Carol Harvey signed on in the early days, and now heads a sales force of 6 people while Sherry concentrates on the creative side of the business.

Carol has decided that she really wants to start a similar business of her own, and has been developing a business plan for her new company on her own time. She continues to do her job well, and does not plan to tell Sherry about her new venture until she is ready to give notice.

Carol is finding that her situation is beginning to create some tough ethical questions for her. She would like to take one of her salespersons, Bill Blake, with her to the new company. Several of her current clients with NPI would come over to the new venture; asking for commitments from them now would significantly ease her attempts at raising startup funds. How much farther can she go while drawing a paycheck from NPI?

DISCUSSION QUESTIONS

1. Is it possible for Carol to be giving her best to NPI in her current frame of mind? Should she continue with NPI once she begins to develop a business plan? Once she has decided that she will probably start her own firm? Once she is definite?

2. Can she ethically discuss her plans with Bill Blake now? Can she begin to negotiate terms of employment with him?

3. Should she approach her current customers for a written commitment to doing business with her new company to present to her banker in confidence? How would you expect her customers to react? How would her banker view such letters?

b. The Survival Stage: Cash-Flow and Performance Measurement

The amount of time required for a new venture to reach profitability is a critical factor in whether or not a business survives the startup trauma. A promising new business, well on its way to viability, can still experience severe cash flow problems; sometimes these can be fatal. Even beyond the startup period, strains on cash can severely limit company growth.

Managers, particularly in survival-stage businesses, track their financial data closely. Most are very conscious of what the income statement tells them, but not enough manage the balance sheet as well. Cash is the foundation for a strong balance sheet. Proper cash management permits the owner to meet the cash needs of the business, take advantage of special buys and discounts, minimize interest expense, and ride out slow periods. A good cash position allows the owner to maintain an adequate level of inventory, replace equipment as needs arise, and to seize expansion opportunities.

Cash demands are often cyclical. On an annual cycle, inventory can be worked down (in essence, partially liquidated) as a slow period approaches, and restocked as the prime selling season returns. On a monthly cycle, the daily balance on the bank statement can show the ebb and flow; a manager can learn clearing times, play the "float," and create inducements for customers to pay in time to fill in "troughs" in the cash balance.

For many businesses, the primary management control on cash is collecting on accounts receivable. Are you in the lending business? Do you mean to be? Carefully screen credit applicants; require a signed application that spells out credit terms. Take immediate action on past-due accounts, and earn a reputation for pursuing defaulters and bad-check artists. Do not be reluctant to cut off those who are beginning to owe you more than they are worth.

Another control is accounts payable management; negotiate extended credit terms where possible, but do not abuse your vendors. Pay promptly when the cash is there, and ask their help when it is not. Other balance sheet items can offer opportunities to improve your cash position. Do you have an "edifice complex?" Has your physical plant exceeded what is business-necessary? Show an expense consciousness, and the attitude will spread to your employees. Clear out dead and excess inventory; there is a cost to carrying it.

Is there a point at which a company's cash position can become too strong? Maintaining a cash balance that far exceeds a comfortable operating cushion in a non-interest-bearing account will certainly drag down the rate of return on our investment. Short and intermediate term excess could be invested temporarily in interest-bearing instruments that can quickly be converted to cash. Longer term excess can require a strategic reevaluation, to consider expansion, diversification, paying down debt, or a huge bonus to the owner.

How can we measure a company's performance relative to these guidelines? While the financial statements give us values for many of the parameters we use as management controls, some relative measures can be even more meaningful. These measures are often expressed as ratios of standard financial statement items. There are several widely used ratios that allow us to compare our performance to norms for our industry.

Minicase 8-2: So, how are we doing so far?

The tax return for Tammany Supply, Inc. for 2014 is complete, and TSI President John Vinturella has decided that it is time to look at some company performance measures. He has routinely calculated some basic percentages, but would like to delve a little deeper this time.

The first two columns of the table below show summaries of the company's Income Statement and Balance Sheet, with some of the key management control variables set off in gray. John would prefer to have a slightly higher gross margin, but the observed 18.7% is satisfactory given their aggressive sales effort; for the past 3 years TSI has posted sales increases over the previous year of 20%+.

The net margin is acceptable, near industry norms published by the American Supply Association, while returns on investment and equity comfortably exceed norms. Collection days, or average days from invoicing to collection, are 20% better (*i.e.* less) than is typical for similar businesses.

The third column represents financial ratios that TSI's accountant suggests that John track. John has calculated the ratios, and we will help him to interpret them following this case. Dun and Bradstreet norms for home supply businesses will add some perspective to our consideration.

Tammany Supply, Inc.

Income:	2014
Sales	$4,362,904
Cost of Goods Sold	$3,545,747
Gross Margin	18.7%
Other Income	$10,813
Total Income	**$827,970**
Expenses:	
Personnel	$379,544
Operations	$174,857
Sales	$51,561
Administration	$98,738
Depreciation	$29,296
Total Expenses	**$733,996**
Profit/Loss BIT	**$93,974**
Taxes	$20,201
Profit/Loss, After tax	$73,773
Net Margin	1.69%
Return on Investment	6.63%

Assets:	2014
Cash	$101,407
Accounts Receivable	$430,486
Collection Days	36.01
Inventory	$326,554
OthCur Assets	$148,312
Total Current Assets	$1,006,759
Total Fixed Assets	$105,713
Total Assets	**$1,112,472**
Liabilities:	
Accounts Payable	$356,320
OthCur Liabilities	$27,777
Net Working Capital	$728,375
Long-Term Debt	$0
Total Liabilities	**$384,097**
Equity	$738,375
Return on Equity	9.99%
Total Liab/Eq	**$1,122,472**

Ratios:	2014 TSI	2014 D&B Norms
Liquidity/Indebtedness		
1 CurAssets/CurDebt	2.62	2.24
2 "Acid Test"	1.77	
3 TotLiab/TotAssets	34.53	
4 CurDebt/TangNetWor	52.0	75.0
5 TotDebt/TangNetWor	52.0	124.7
6 CurDebt/Inventory	117.6	81.2
Sales/Profitability		
7 NetSales/TangNetWor	5.91	3.84
8 NetSales/NetWkCap	7.01	5.39
9 NetSales/Inventory	13.4	4.5
10 NetProf/NetSales	1.69	1.58
11 NetProf/TangNetWor	9.99	7.29
12 NetProf/NetWkCap	11.85	8.66
Other Normed		
13 FxAssets/TangNetWor	14.3	32.8
14 Inventory/NetWkCap	44.8	93.3

JOHN B. VINTURELLA, PH.D.

DISCUSSION QUESTIONS

1. How applicable are norms for an entire industry to a specific small business? Are differences from norms more reflective of quality of management, operating strategies, or competitive conditions?
2. Is rapid increase in sales volume a valid reason for a low gross margin? What is the mechanism by which this occurs? Does an acceptable net margin validate this approach?
3. Does a return on equity of about 10% represent an effective use of our personal resources? What are our options, and what is their likely return?

The following discussion of financial ratios references the table in the previous case.

(1) Liquidity and Indebtedness (Indicators of financial stability and leverage)

The liquidity of a firm indicates its ability to meet cash requirements, ride out difficult times, and expand in good times. Ratio 1, current assets to current liabilities, is a widely used measure of liquidity referred to as the current ratio. Ratio 2, the "acid-test" is thought to be a better measure because it uses current assets less inventory (generally our least liquid current asset). Ratio 3 shows total liabilities to be less than 35% of total assets. Based on norms, TSI seems to be comparatively liquid. What would illiquidity convey? What are ways of improving liquidity?

Another measure of the financial stability of a firm is its use of indebtedness, sometimes referred to as its financial leverage. Ratio 4 shows current debt as 52% of tangible net worth, or equity. Ratio 5 shows total debt to equity the same as current, since there is no long-term debt. Ratio 6, current debt to inventory, is high relative to norms. Is this inconsistent with the previous ratios? Do we need more information? Is this more of an indicator of TSI's rapid inventory turnover?

The comparisons to norms indicate that TSI is not very leveraged. Is this a positive or a negative? Should TSI borrow $250,000 to be more in line with norms? What might it do with the money?

(2) Sales and Profitability (Indicators of performance)

Ratios 7 and 8 show that TSI is getting a good sales yield on its equity and its working capital. Ratio 9 is a tangible measure of its rapid inventory turnover, triple the industry norm! Combined with earlier indicators, should TSI borrow to increase its inventory? Do we know if their level of inventory is holding the business back? Should they consider a greater depth of existing inventory, or additional product lines? What market factors would determine their actions?

The profitability measures in ratios 10, 11, and 12 also comfortably exceed norms. These represent, respectively, the percentage of each sales dollar that TSI brings to the "bottom line," its return on equity, and its working capital growth rate. What do these ratios say about TSI as an investment? What types of management actions produce these results?

(3) Analysis and Conclusions

Ratios 13 and 14 offer two more normed indicators of TSI performance. Fixed assets are a relatively low percentage of equity, indicating that investment in vehicles and equipment could reasonably be considered. Inventory is less than half the norm as a percent of working capital.

What does all of this tell us? Is TSI management too conservative about debt? What might happen to the positive indicators on sale and profits were they to get more leverage? Are we using the ratios properly by assuming deviation from the norm is indicative of a problem? Has John developed a strategy that provides a comfortable living while making it easy to sleep nights? Is that all bad?

c. Success: Going for the Growth

Many entrepreneurs' primary interest is in building a "lifestyle" business, that is, one which provides them a living (in varying degrees of comfort) while allowing them to do what they want to do. Other entrepreneurs want to take the business as far as it can go. Decision time comes when the business works its way through the startup trauma to achieving some degree of stability.

Every business, committed to rapid growth or not, should always have a business plan in place that is updated annually. Even if our basic business does not change, our market does, the competitive environment does, and innovation and technology create more options for the consumer. All the arguments in favor of the business plan for the startup venture apply equally to the ongoing business.

In the annual revision of the business plan, market and environmental data must be updated, and the strategic plan revisited and frequently revised. Actual financial data for the year recently completed must be compared with what was projected, and future projections adjusted accordingly. Reasons for deviations must be identified and addressed.

(1) How and where do we grow?

Strategic options in a growth situation must be identified. Can we improve market share in the current market? Should we try to sell more to current customers by widening our product line? Can we cover a broader geographic area? Are there other channels of distribution that should be considered? Is our business concept franchisable? Should we develop a branch office network? How big can we get to be? How fast can we get there?

This process is very similar to startup; we must do rigorous market research, clearly identify the specific market we will serve, formulate a strategy that effectively seizes the perceived opportunity, and develop financial projections to measure our progress.

(2) International Opportunities

As we consider our geographic span of operations, most small business owners think only in terms of domestic markets.

International opportunities, they reason, are the province of the large corporations; "multinational company" has come to be synonymous with "huge company." Typical reactions to suggestions of evaluating international markets include: "I don't have the time to deal with all the complications;" "there are too many ways to get burned; "there are enough opportunities in the U.S. (Canada, etc.)."

Trade agreements are minimizing the complications and the dangers; Export Assistance Centers are opening around the U.S.; advances in telecommunications are shrinking distances and bringing us closer and closer to the truly global economy. Market information relative to global markets is improving in availability and timeliness.

d. Disengagement

For the successful business, alternative paths for the future of the firm may be considered to be the pursuit of growth, or merely "holding one's own." A case could be made for there being a middle road of accepting some evolutionary growth within the current market and product offerings.

The standing-still option is generally associated with disengagement on the part of the entrepreneur. Perhaps the everyday struggles and aggravations of the business have worn them down. Or the success they have achieved may seem sufficient, whereas its expansion does not appear satisfying. Perhaps they are simply bored of doing essentially the same thing for an extended period of time.

Frequently, what drives the disengagement process is a new focus on personal fulfillment. Many disengaged business owners seek a calmer life and greater family involvement. Many actively participate in community activities, and in teaching. Others go back to school or lose themselves in their hobbies.

Of course, the ultimate disengagement is to shut the business down, or sell it; in the case of most family businesses, giving the reins to a successor is another option.

(1) Is it time to go?

There comes a time in the life of every business owner when he or she begins to entertain the thought of leaving the business. There can be many reasons for deciding that it may be time to move on, but they tend to fall into one of three categories: business reasons; transitional issues, or; life-stage issues.

Business reasons for moving on are not confined to failing companies; often concern about the company's inability to grow for lack of capital, or marginal returns from the business, can lead a person to consider other options. Sometimes the return on the owner's business investment would be greater from passive instruments, such as mutual funds, with more security and less stress. If no action is taken under these circumstances, the static or marginal business can become a business at risk, and options are more limited.

Transitional issues can relate to the company's ability to compete in a business that is changing rapidly, or concern about the costs of adapting to the changes required to stay competitive in that environment. Another difficult transitional issue can be a change in the ownership structure or conflicts among owners; often the only resolution is for one or more owners to sell their stake, or to liquidate the business entirely. The loss of key personnel, or some critical skill, or general workforce unrest can lead a business owner to decide that it is easier to move on than to ride out the difficulty.

Even with all going well in the business, however, issues related to the owner's life stage can raise the issue of moving on. The small business owner is president of the company the day the business opens, with no room for promotion except to "retired." If the company reaches a growth plateau, the owner's duties can become rather monotonous, and well beneath his or her abilities.

In many cases, it simply becomes time to retire, either for reasons of age or loss of enthusiasm. In family businesses, a reluctance to move on can severely retard the development of the next generation, and under-utilize valuable management resources.

Retirement can be a particularly touchy issue because many business owners equate it with death. It is a violation of the person's work ethic, and their very identity and role in life. Consideration of retirement also brings some of the owner's unspoken fears to the surface. Many have not adequately planned for life after work, either financially, or by the development of other interests. In family businesses, there is frequently the concern that the next generation is not up to the challenge.

(2) Preparing to Leave the Business

There are three basic levels of planning for leaving a business: no planning needed, it will take care of itself; a one-step plan, namely sell and forget about it, and; an orderly longer-term approach. What are the risks of the two lower-level approaches?

Chances of receiving the greatest long-term return on our business investment are greatest with thoughtful advance planning. If the business is to be sold, it can be conditioned for enhanced value.

In a family business, we must determine whether there is or will be a suitable successor, possibly after a period of non-family business leadership. If so, the grooming process, transferring responsibility from leader to successor generation, should begin early enough to proceed gradually. If there is not a suitable successor on the horizon, then planning for selling the business may be the best option.

Conditioning a business for sale is similar to getting a house ready to sell. We must truthfully prepare a good case for the property's benefits for a purchaser, and present the property at its best. A professional evaluator can help us with a realistic asking price, and their experience could help them identify improvements worth making to maximize our eventual selling price.

Our sales presentation should include "recast" financial statements that make the statements more "owner-neutral". Closely-held companies often understate earnings in some way to minimize taxes; prospective buyers are more interested in maximizing profits.

Ways to improve the business' presentation include getting rid of obsolete inventory, upgrading equipment, and general housekeeping. Business appraisers can help identify other areas for improvement, and suggest a range for asking price.

(3) Evaluating the Business

Our most effective tool in selling the business is a realistic view of what it is worth to a "stranger." This requires a dispassionate look at the "story" behind the numbers in the financial statement. This process was discussed at some length in Chapter 2 from the prospective buyer's point of view; the following checklist overlaps that material somewhat, but leans more toward the seller's perspective:

Adjusted Book Value

| Accounts Receivable: | Allow a reasonable amount for bad and questionable debt. |
| Inventory: | Allow for obsolete, and damaged goods, and for overstock. |

Equipment:	Deduct unusable; use replacement value for remainder.
Accounts Payable:	Resolve disputed amounts owed and service charges.
Other:	Have any business property and investments appraised
	Recognize accruals (taxes, insurance payments, etc.)
	Prepare payment schedules on all notes payable and receivable.

Earnings Issues, "Goodwill"

Salaries:	Estimate owner-neutral compensation.
Performance:	Compare to lender guidelines, industry norms.
Contracts:	Estimate whether each adds or subtracts value.
Personnel:	Estimate cost to new owner if key personnel leave.
Other:	Estimate value of patents, logos, and trademarks.

Strategic Issues

Strategic issues are the least tangible, and the hardest to relate to the value of the company. Some of the questions that the owner should consider are:

- Is our market share large enough to be significant, small enough to allow growth?

- Is the competitive climate favorable to the future of the business?
- Are there any legal or technological trends impacting the future of the industry?
- Will cultural or demographic trends help or hurt future prospects?
- Can I point out growth opportunities to the new owner?
- Does my departure affect the distinctive competence of the business?

(4) Marketing the Business

Once a thorough review of issues related to company value is conducted, we are ready to put together a sales brochure, where the business is described in general terms without being identified; this is a marketing tool for distribution and listing to attract genuine prospects. We also need to prepare a detailed business presentation package, with background information and financial data, to give in confidence to those who express interest.

While the business presentation package has many elements in common with a business plan, its thrust is considerably different. There is no need to sell the management team, since it is essentially the management team to whom we are presenting it. Strategic possibilities may be outlined, but the chosen strategy will, of course, be determined by the new ownership.

Typical elements of the business presentation package are:

History of the business, significant strategic changes, emerging trends.

Company facilities and methods of operation.
Major customers, key suppliers, and competitive climate.
Current marketing practices, and promising possibilities.
Evaluation of human resources available to new owners.
Financial data and projections.

Once this information is assembled, and presented in its most sales-oriented manner, we can begin to prospect for buyers. A business opportunity ad in the local newspaper or business publication, or the Wall Street Journal, can quickly generate inquiries, but most will probably just be "tire kickers." Another disadvantage of this approach is that it will quickly be "on the street" that the business is for sale, and this could have a negative effect on employees and important customers.

Trade sources and associations reach a narrower but more appropriate audience, and generally can qualify prospects in a discretionary manner. These prospects will often include your competitors; while they might be serious prospects, there is some danger to advanced negotiations, as you reveal financial details and possibly a list of key customers. Many owners offer their businesses through brokers. Larger businesses will sometimes work through merger and acquisition specialists.

Negotiations with serious prospects can focus as much on payment terms as on selling price. Be prepared to be asked to finance part of the purchase.

(5) Passing the Business to the Next Generation

Let us briefly review the process of grooming a successor (see Chapter 4). Once the successor is chosen, the training and development process begins. Authority and responsibility are gradually shifted from the lead to the next generation. The lead generation must allow the next to use their authority, even when the lead disagrees. The most successful transitions occur on a timetable, and with a new role assigned to the lead to limit interference with the new direction the company might take.

(6) Remaining a Productive Member of Society

The displaced owner generally has several options available once the current business is successfully sold or "handed off." Many take the resources generated, and plow them into another business or new venture. Some treat it as semi-retirement, remaining with the business in some lesser capacity, part-time or consultory.

The most "successful" retirees seem to be those who developed other interests while working, and pursue them in retirement. This could be through a "regular" job, doing something they really enjoy, with the lower stress level of employee rather than owner. Those whose financial security is assured might perform civic and volunteer activities, or catch up on their travel.

Summary

Getting the doors open on a new venture is only the first in a series of challenges on the way to entrepreneurial success.

In many cases, the second (often termed "survival") stage of business development, *i.e.*, solidifying the viability of the business, can be even more difficult.

A cornerstone of the successful long-term business is a commitment to ethical behavior, community involvement, and social responsibility. This commitment is tested while working for others, as we consider starting our own ventures, and on the way we treat our employees. The rewards of keeping this commitment can far exceed the monetary rewards of a successful business.

Another key to business success is to carefully monitor performance, and to act on the information this process yields. Newer businesses are particularly vulnerable to problems of cash flow, as the requirements of a growing business place continual demands on today's resources. Entrepreneurs must manage the balance sheet, particularly cash and receivables, as well as the income statement, that is, the instinctive focus on sales volume. Relationships between financial statement values, in the form of ratios and percentages, can be compared to industry norms as a way of "grading" ourselves.

Once a business reaches a level of stability and prosperity that may be considered "success," the entrepreneur is at a crossroads. Many continue on a growth pattern, expanding the business in a variety of ways, sometimes even becoming international. Others become disengaged, often to the point of shutting down or selling the business.

Whatever path is chosen, the actions of the entrepreneur should always be guided by a current, well-researched, and considered business plan.

Review Questions

1. What are the stages in small business growth? How can we tell which we are currently in?
2. Why is ethical behavior important to a business? Can we identify ethical attitudes of businesses with which we are familiar? Can we identify ethical challenges we have faced in our business experience?
3. Why is cash flow so important to the growing business? What can we do to improve the cash flow of such a business? Can cash position ever be too strong?
4. How are the commonly used financial ratios helpful in managing a business?
5. What are the common strategic options in growing a business? How do we choose between them? What are the primary limitants?
6. Why would a business owner not pursue a growth strategy?

Case Study 8-1   Tammany Supply, Inc. (E)

INTRODUCTION

The oil price collapse of the mid-2000s took a heavy toll on the Louisiana economy. In western St. Tammany parish, an upscale suburb of New Orleans which had been experiencing explosive growth, new residential construction fell dramatically. For Tammany Supply, Inc. (TSI), a Covington plumbing wholesaler serving that market, sales fell 40% from 2004 to 2007.

With the assistance of a broader product line, including the opening of a patio furniture store, a modest recovery in TSI's fortunes occurred from 2008 to 2010 (see the "D" case). Confident that the company was back on solid ground, TSI president John Vinturella began scaling back his business duties and pursuing some local academic opportunities.

By the fall of 2011, Vinturella was down to a day a week in Covington, as TSI's general manager, Ron Stewart, had risen to the occasion. In the fall of 2012, John's son-in-law, Scott Olson, joined the company and expressed interest in one day running the operation. With Scott as Ron's right-hand man, Vinturella felt comfortable in separating even further from the business.

THE RECOVERY ACCELERATES

A building boom began in mid-2012. TSI sales for 2012 increased 20% over 2011. By the spring of 2013 homebuilding had become so lively that the company decided to sell its patio furniture store to an employee. By shedding this operation, the company had undone much of the diversification it had undertaken in the late 2000s, and returned to its roots. TSI was now at least as heavily dependent on new residential construction in western St. Tammany as it had ever been.

But that was not a bad place to be. TSI sales in 2013 increased another 30% over 2012 sales, exceeding $3.5 million for the first time; profits were likewise the highest in company history. In 2014, sales rose another 24%, exceeding $4 million, and profits decreased only slightly (see Figure 8-1).

CLOUDS ON THE HORIZON

By the end of 2014, local builders were beginning to catch up with the demand, indicating a levelling off of building activity, but at a comfortable plateau. The boom was running its course, but there certainly did not seem to be a crash in sight.

There were ways, however, in which this situation felt different from the prosperity of the early 2000s. TSI's early success was accelerated by the high-end nature of the St. Tammany housing industry; their clientele bought luxury goods, with their attendant luxurious profit margins. In the 2010's, most of the housing being built was middle-range and below; margins were skimpy, and TSI had to move a lot more material to make as much profit.

The competitive situation also felt different. The regional plumbing supply chain which had opened a branch in the market in 2011 seemed to be there to stay, despite its inability to take a significant share of business from TSI. Another chain operator was making serious noises about joining the competition in western St. Tammany. As the market had gone a bit down-scale, TSI was becoming more vulnerable to the low-price, low-service sales approach of the larger companies. The resultant discomfort was intensified by the announcement of a Home Depot being built just 2 miles south of TSI.

RELATED DEVELOPMENTS

Figure 8-1

As John Vinturella, TSI president, looked at the 2014 sales reports, he thought what a hardened pessimist he must be. Despite two record-breaking years in a row, he was feeling burned out on business, and dreading the prospect of facing another economic cycle, mild though it seemed.

From 2006 to 2008, Vinturella had worked on a personal-investment diversification program to supplement the one he directed at TSI. He seeded the startup of a microbrewery, then sold his stake to seed a "cajun food" manufacturer. He bought a computer consulting firm and merged it with the software company used by TSI. He and his brothers opened a quick-oil-change franchise in New Orleans. Vinturella was positioned to prosper when the area economy recovered.

While the area economy had found bottom in 2007, it merely bounced along that bottom for the next few years. Vinturella overestimated the pace of recovery, and experienced another "crash," this time in his personal finances, beginning in 2010. Investments from ten years earlier had started to become drains on cash. The recent investments were taking longer to reach profitability than projected.

Vacancies in the TSI building were causing tremendous strains in making mortgage payments. An orderly shutdown of these ventures was begun, climaxing in 2012 when Vinturella returned his building to the bank.

Because of his personal financial reverses, TSI had become Vinturella's only significant asset. The thought of cashing out entered his mind; were he to sell now, at a peak, he would probably be able to live off the proceeds for life.

DECISION TIME

From his early 2015 perspective, Vinturella observes that he is little-needed at TSI and that suits him fine. At 52 years old, he is ready to formalize his separation from the business. Ron is also 52, and should be around for 15 more years. Scott, 30 years old, is progressing nicely in the business, and showing leadership potential.

In 2013, Vinturella's outside income exceeded his TSI income. In 2014, outside income fell off a bit, increasing his reliance on the TSI draw. A moderately large consulting contract was expected in early 2015 that would support him through the summer, but there was nothing certain for the rest of the year yet.

Vinturella figured that investing the proceeds of the sale of the company would provide as much income as he was drawing from the company now, without any of the worries of the business. He enjoyed his outside activities far more than his TSI duties.

He reached into his file drawer, and pulled out the folder marked "Selling the Business." It contained a letter from a business brokerage service offering to list his business for sale, and a prospectus on an electrical supply house for sale that he thought could serve as a model for his listing.

But on the other hand ...

STUDY QUESTIONS

1. Is now a good time to sell, or do prospective buyers see the same danger signs that Vinturella sees? Should he approach the firm currently considering entering the market? Can he get that firm and his current competitor into a "bidding war?"
2. Are the danger signs real or imagined? Is Vinturella just getting "gun-shy" from his earlier reverses? Would a levelling off at this sales volume adversely affect TSI's profitability?

3. Were some of Vinturella's recent decisions those of a short-termer? Was the reversal of the diversification program short-sighted? Has the market matured to the point where TSI has lost the competitive advantage of being the small, independent, locally owned firm?

4. Is it smart for Vinturella to consider selling now, when his alternate sources of income are not yielding much, or should he wait until his other pursuits prove more profitable? Is it fair for him to continue to draw a substantial salary? What do you see happening to TSI's market value if he waits a year or two to offer it for sale?

5. Assuming that the business might appraise for a million dollars, how much might Vinturella realize from its sale? What kind of income might that provide for life? What would the investment options be? Does he owe anything to his children?

6. What are Vinturella's *real* reasons for considering a sale of the business? Could his sense of no longer being needed be driving it, or is it for business reasons? How might Ron and Scott react if he brought them into discussing the possibility?

7. Were Vinturella to decide not to sell, are there any dangers in prolonging the current situation? Might other employees perceive it as a disinterested leader, caretaker manager, not-yet-ready successor designate? Do they care? Is it an accurate perception? How might customers and suppliers view the situation? What about competitors?

8. Can Vinturella really be the company leader on a one-day-a-week schedule? Even with his loss of interest? Are there any actions he can take, short of selling, to pass on the leadership of TSI? Can a non-owner manager be a leader? How soon can Scott take over? When should he? What are the criteria?

CONCLUSIONS

Can entrepreneurship be taught? In the broadest sense of the term, the answer is probably no. Peter Drucker disagrees, saying that "it is systematic work."

Many of the skills of successful entrepreneurs can be taught, and sensitivity to business opportunity can be sharpened. A thorough and orderly approach to business planning allows us to assess whether an opportunity exists, and to chart the best way to take maximum advantage of that opportunity. From there, a hardy individual can decide, with a little less uncertainty, whether or not to pursue that opportunity.

The concepts of entrepreneurship cannot be absorbed passively; they are based on powers of observation and critical thinking, development of skills in estimating and projecting economic results, and the integration and application of knowledge from coursework, life experience, and attempts at understanding human nature.

The Internet will almost certainly be your primary source of information, but you may wish to follow stories in the newspaper and periodicals where the subject bears on the business in which you are interested. These might be about business incubators, funding of ventures, and success stories. These will keep you current in the field and will often add depth to your understanding.

The process of creating or seizing an opportunity is less the result of a deliberate search than it is a mindset of maintaining a form of vigilance that is sensitized to business opportunity. This frequently relates to the prospective entrepreneur's current profession or interests, where he or she perceives a process that can be more efficiently performed an attractive new service or improvement of an existing service, or some business or geographic "niche" that is being underserved.

"An opportunity is attractive, durable, and timely and is anchored in a product or service that creates or adds value for its buyer or end user. Opportunities are created because there are changing circumstances, inconsistencies, chaos, lags, or leads, information gaps, and a variety of other vacuums, and because there are entrepreneurs who can recognize and seize them." (Source: Jeff Timmons, *New Venture Creation*)

Obviously, no opportunity is a sure thing, even though the path to riches has been described as, simply "...you make some stuff, sell it for more than it cost you... that's all there is except for a few million details." The devil is in those details, and if one is not prepared to accept the possibility of failure, one should not attempt a business start-up.

Entire books are devoted to the subject of why small businesses fail, but the reason is generally one, or a combination, of the following: *inadequate financing* often due to overly optimistic sales projections; *management shortcomings*, including inadequate financial controls, lax customer credit, inexperience, and neglect, and; *misreading the market*, often indicated by a failure to reach the "critical mass" required in sales volume and profitability due to competitive disadvantages or general industry weakness.

The Internet is an outstanding medium for the research required to build a solid business plan. Starting your business with such a plan greatly improves the chances for success.

Beyond its use as a research tool, the Internet can be a business platform. Many new businesses are "virtual," that is, exist only in "cyberspace." The capital requirements for a new business where there is no "bricks and mortar" presence are considerably lessened. This can even allow the entrepreneur to initially work from home.

Lifehack (http://www.lifehack.org/articles/money/7-reasons-why-you-should-start-your-own-internet-business.html) suggests some of the types of businesses that you can start on the Internet:

- Sell your handmade arts and crafts on Etsy
- Run an informative site that generates revenue through advertisements
- Provide professional services to clients around the world
- Generate client leads for offline businesses
- Sell other peoples' products and earn a commission for each referral

In the age of the Internet there are few businesses that can afford not to be on the "World-Wide Web," the popular graphic interface to the "net." A web presence, through a web site, is the "business card" of the Internet age. People generally find a site via search engines such as Google (google.com).

Once you have a web presence the challenge is to be noticed. The primary way to improve your chances is to use a technique called "search engine optimization," or SEO. Other ways to drive visitors to your site are social media and pay-per-click (PPC) advertising.

With social media you build a network of friends and your communications include them. Most social media accounts are free, but they also sell advertising.

Facebook is a platform for a web page and the best-known and biggest social network on the Web. The number of users is said to be more than 1.5 billion active users around the world. Thus your Facebook page makes your business truly global. Other social media include Twitter, Pinterest, and Instagram.

PPC is a model of internet marketing in which advertisers pay a fee each time one of their ads is clicked. Essentially, it's a way of buying visits to your site, rather than attempting to "earn" those visits "organically."

Market research is vital to planning for any new venture. Among the questions one might ask are the following:

Who are our customers? Where are they? How are they best reached?

What are they buying? From whom? Why? What are their price expectations?

How big is the market? How large a market share can I capture?"

How intense is the competition? What are their advantages/ disadvantages?

How is the product distributed, marketed? How are prices set and changed?

Most of your research will be done on the Internet, but do not overlook other sources. Census data, particularly demographic information for your market area, can often be useful. Trade sources for your particular industry can give you a greater feel for how such business is conducted.

With the information gathered in the research phase, we can refine our business concept further by considering our "marketing mix," those decisions to be made for our marketing plan that are generally referred to as the "four P's:" We will take a first pass at the following decisions to continue our screening, then refine the answers for the business plan.

(1) Product

What is the product that the market needs? How well positioned are we to provide it? How will we differentiate ourselves from the competition?

What brand name and packaging will we use? How wide will our product line be? What will be its features, accessories and options?

(2) Price

Will our price be competition-based or quality-image-based? What is the range of pricing options? How price-sensitive are sales? Can we be low cost <u>and</u> high service?

What will our terms be? What discounts and allowances will we provide?

(3) Promotion

How will we promote the product? What aspects of the product should we stress? How and where will we advertise? What are the most cost-effective media? Can we afford an agency?

Are there some non-traditional promotional methods which could be effective? Does our venture lend itself to personal selling over mass-marketing, cross-promotions with related products? Are there opportunities for free publicity?

(4) Place

Where and how will we distribute the product? What will the distribution "channel" look like?

Once we have made the marketing decisions we can move to determining for the business, as we have structured it, how it might fare in the marketplace. Projecting how much we might sell in the initial stages of the business is a bit daunting, but is critical to a determination of the profitability of a venture.

Breakeven analysis is a good way to develop a sense of the feasibility of a venture. It is a way to determine what level of sales is required to allow the venture to generate just enough "margin dollars" to cover its expenses. Margin is the amount of money left over after the cost of the goods sold is deducted.

Breakeven analysis may be considered a screening device. Once an opportunity passes the "screen test," we must then evaluate whether there might be an alternative to starting a new business. In some product areas, the chances for success are enhanced by acquiring a franchise. In some cases, purchase of an existing business can avoid the start-up trauma, while eliminating a competitor.

Many entrepreneurs choose to work at home. This could be to conduct an online business, or it could be a modest start for a business that they are hoping to expand into a physical presence when finances allow.

Think about what services you can offer online. First think freelance. Are you a skilled web developer? Do you have writing talent? Are you a creative graphics designer? Are you good at online research? Are you fluent enough to be a translator?

An alternative to starting your own business is purchasing a franchise. A franchise is a continuing relationship between a franchisor and a franchisee in which the franchisor's *knowledge, image, success, manufacturing, and marketing techniques* are supplied to the franchisee for a consideration. This consideration usually consists of a high "up-front" fee, and a significant royalty percentage, which generally require a fairly long time to recover.

Franchising offers those who lack business experience (but do not lack capital) a business with a good probability of success. It is a ready-made business, with all the incentives of a small business combined with the management skills of a large one. It is a way to be "in business for yourself, not by yourself."

The advantages can be considerable. The franchise fee buys instant product recognition built and maintained by sophisticated advertising and marketing programs. The franchisor's management experience and depth assists the franchisee by providing employee guidelines, policies and procedures, operating experience, and sometimes even financial assistance. They provide proven methods for determining promising locations, and a successful store design and equipment configuration. Centralized purchasing gives large-buyer "clout" to each location.

The large initial cost can be difficult to raise. The highly structured environment can be more limiting than it is reassuring. Continuing royalty costs take a significant portion of profits. Several small business periodicals evaluate and rank franchise opportunities. There are now several franchise "matchmaking" firms who can assist in the evaluation process.

How do you choose among all the available franchises? Does it complement your interests? Even if you hire someone to manage the business, expect to spend a lot of time with the operation. Is the name well known? If not, what are you paying for? Is the fee structure reasonable, and all costs clearly described?

Is the franchisor professional? Evaluate them on the clarity of the agreement, and how well your rights are protected, the strength of their training and support program, and their commitment to your success. Be sure to talk to current franchisees about their experiences. Beware of a franchisor committed to a rate of growth that exceeds their ability to manage; they may not be sufficiently interested in the sales they have already made.

Is a franchise a sure path to instant riches? Is it the only hope for independent firms in today's market? Does the franchise deliver business that we might not have gotten anyway? Is it really entrepreneurship; did I go into business or did my money?

Another alternative to a startup is to buy an existing business. To some extent, buying a business is less risky because its operating history provides meaningful data on its chances of success under our concept. We must, however, balance the acquisition cost against what the cost of a startup might have been.

One important factor is the seller's reasons for offering the business for sale. Often these are for personal and career reasons, such as a readiness to retire with the absence of a successor, or another opportunity perceived as a better fit. Where there are business reasons for selling, such as personnel problems, or inability to stand up to the competition, we must decide whether all that is missing is a quality of management that we can provide, or that there are some changes we can make in the way the business is operated that will make the difference.

Due diligence must be performed before a binding offer is made. Is the company's history and network of business relationships clear? Are their financial statements representative? What do they say about the business? Are there any unstated dangers or risks? Are there any hidden liabilities? Often, a review of the financials by our banker and accountant can be valuable.

How "good" an organization is it? How is it perceived by its customers and suppliers? If we do not buy it, how tough a competitor will it be? What will be the effect of an ownership change on the customer base, supplier relations, etc.? How much customer loyalty is to the business, and how much to the current owner?

Does the company have a "niche?" Is it the one in which you want to operate? Is there a competitive advantage to the operation that is sustainable? Are its assets useful to you? Will key personnel remain with the business?

If the decision is made that purchase of an existing business could improve our chances for success, we must then evaluate existing businesses to determine whether any are available at a price that is economically more favorable than a new venture. How do we value a business?

Before examining specific techniques for business evaluation, it must be emphasized that there is no one correct value for a business. Any valuation is based on assumptions, and projections of future performance. As in our breakeven analysis discussion, discomfort about basing financial decisions on assumptions and projections is natural.

Entrepreneurship requires exploring uncharted territory, and operating in an environment of uncertainty. Success depends on applying our best judgment to reducing that uncertainty.

The most difficult issue in small business sales is establishing a selling price. It is an inexact science, characterized by a seller's too-high expectations, and an overly skeptical prospective buyer.

One method of evaluating a business is the market approach, basing the value of the business on projections of earnings multiplied by a typical price/earnings ratio (P/E) for the industry. Company history is often a guide to generating sales projections. It will probably take some research to find an appropriate P/E.

The earnings approach to valuing a business views the business as one more option for investing our money, that is, given our assessment of the risk involved, we have a certain expectation of return. We would certainly expect a greater return than on securities backed by the U.S. Treasury, but would possibly accept a lesser return than on a highly speculative venture.

The book-value of a corporation is generally shown on its balance sheet as "Net Worth," or "Owner's Equity." It represents the excess value of the company's assets over its liabilities. This assumes that all components of the balance sheet are fairly valued, and that the assets are useful to the new owner's mission. Book-value sales are almost always based on adjustments to the balance sheet.

If we decide we want to buy a business, we should decide on a bargaining range before we go into the final negotiating session. If we cannot meet on price, perhaps concessions on payment terms could make up the difference. We should know the tax and legal consequences of our options. If the discussion takes us outside our range, we should schedule another session, and reanalyze the data. We must allow for the possibility that the deal cannot be made.

Ultimately we must decide whether the purchase, at a price that the seller will accept, gives us a better chance of success than starting from scratch in competition with the business.

Whatever form your venture might take, a business plan greatly improves your chance of success. The purpose of a business plan is to recognize and define a business opportunity, describe how that opportunity will be seized by the management team, and to demonstrate that the business is feasible and worth the effort.

Where implementation of the plan requires participation of lenders and/or investors, the plan must also clearly and convincingly communicate the financial proposal to the prospective stakeholders: how much you need from them, what kind of return they can expect, and how they can be paid back.

A well-conceived business plan can serve as a management tool to settle major policy issues, identify "keys to success," establish goals and check-points, and consider long-term prospects.

Who is the audience for it? Certainly, the plan is very useful if we are looking for investors or lenders. It is the primary tool used to convince prospective stakeholders that the idea is promising, the market is accessible, the firm's management is capable, serious and disciplined, and that the return on investment is attractive. But even if we can finance the venture ourselves, these are useful issues to address.

While the formats of business plans can be as varied as the businesses themselves, there are components that should appear in all plans. These include an executive summary, elements which describe the opportunity, elements which specify how the business will operate, an analysis of financial expectations, a closing summary, and any supporting documentation.

Within the plan for the overall business are several sub-plans. One is the strategic plan.

The foundation for the strategic plan is a clear mission statement for the venture. This statement can be developed by addressing the following questions:

What business am I in? The answer to this question is not as simple as it seems. A good example of an industry group that failed to take a broader view is the railroads. If they had viewed their business as transportation rather than *trains-and-tracks,* then there would be airlines named *Union Pacific* and *Illinois Central.*

Other questions useful to mission development include: Whom is our product intended to satisfy? What customer needs are being satisfied? How are these needs being satisfied, that is, by which of our methods or products?

An important strategic option is in how we price our product (as a price leader, value leader, or prestige product). Other options include the way in which we differentiate ourselves from the competition, and the particular subset of the market, or niche, we seek to serve.

The major strength of a company is that which most clearly distinguishes it from the competition, referred to as its "distinctive competence." It can take many forms, but it must be identified and built upon. This competitive advantage can be in a primary aspect of the business (manufacture, sales, service), or a secondary one (support, personnel, purchasing, etc.). It is the critical factor in the company's value-adding process.

Another major sub-plan is the financial plan.

Once we develop a sales forecast we have determined the scale of the business. The forecast determines the amount of people, space and equipment the venture will require which in turn can be related to financial requirements.

The financial plan is usually expressed in a "pro forma" financial statement. Pro Forma is Latin for ""as a matter of form," but indicates before the fact rather than historic financial statements. The income statement is the key indicator of the potential of the business.

The income section of the income statement shows the sales estimate and cost of goods sold (CGS), and the difference - generally referred to as gross margin dollars, or margin. CGS is generally expressed as a percentage of sales. Margin dollars are then available to pay expenses, with the remainder being the before-tax profit.

Categories for the expense section of the statement can be grouped into: personnel; administrative; sales expense, and; operations. Methods of allocation between these groups can vary widely, but this structure is useful for considering the form our expenses will take.

Personnel expenses consist of salaries (often split into "Officers" and "Others") and related costs, such as payroll taxes and benefits. These costs are sometimes apportioned to the other groups based on personnel functions.

Administrative costs can include accounting and legal expenses, bad debt and collection costs, bank charges, depreciation, and interest. Estimation of interest paid is iterative, that is, the amount to be borrowed must be estimated, yielding a number for interest expense; this is part of the profit/loss picture, which determines how much must be borrowed. Seldom are more than 2 or 3 passes required to converge to a final estimate, and spreadsheet programs make the process simple.

Sales expenses include advertising and promotion, and sales commissions. Operations costs are such things as rent, vehicle expense, utilities, and supplies.

In building a spreadsheet *pro forma* income statement, we are building a "model" of the business. It should be constructed using relationships rather than constant values, such as margin and some expense categories as a percent of sales, sales increases with time as a percentage growth, etc. Then we can experiment with a range of reasonable alternatives for our "control variables," such as estimated sales, and profit margins.

Another statement is the balance sheet which shows the value of the company at a point in time (opening day, end of the fiscal year). This value is expressed as the value of the company's assets, and its liabilities, with the difference being net worth or owners' equity.

Assets are classified as "Current" or "Other." Current assets include cash and "liquid" investments such as certificates of deposit, and items (relatively) readily converted to cash, such as inventory and accounts receivable. Often the values presented account for a portion of inventory being obsolete, and a portion of accounts receivable being uncollectible, but this is not applicable to startup ventures. Other assets are primarily "Fixed," that is, have some relatively long service life over which their value is amortized. These include property and improvements, vehicles, and equipment. Depreciation schedules are generally "aggressive," taking maximum advantage of tax law, and frequently cause fixed asset values to be understated.

Liabilities are generally classified as "Current" and "Long-Term." Current liabilities consist of items due in the relatively short term, such as accruals of sales and payroll taxes, and

"Accounts Payable," or invoices for goods received. Long-term liabilities are generally "Notes Payable" with fixed repayment terms.

The difference between assets and liabilities, as though the company were being liquidated, is the net worth of the business, or "Owners' Equity." The balance sheet must be consistent with the income statement. Accumulated profits become gain in equity, purchases become assets, note payments decrease loan balances, and depreciation reduces asset values.

The capital requirements of the business can be developed as the sum of: pre-startup outlay; fixed assets needed within the startup period, and; accumulated operating losses until break-even or better is achieved. The requirement is generally met by some combination of cash and loans.

A fairly new way of funding a venture is by "crowdfunding."

Crowdfunding makes use of the easy accessibility of vast networks of friends, family and colleagues through social media websites like Facebook, Twitter and LinkedIn to get the word out about a new business and attract investors. Crowdfunding has the potential to increase entrepreneurship by expanding the pool of investors from whom funds can be raised beyond the traditional circle of owners, relatives and venture capitalists.

The benefits of crowdfunding include the following:

- **Access to capital.** In many instances, you may not even have to give up equity. Some funding may simply be donations. Other investors may just require early access to the product you are developing.
- **Risk reduction.** There are no loans to repay, no collateral to pledge.
- **Marketing advantages.** The public is made aware of your product early in the process. Even those who do not invest become potential customers.

The traditional means of funding ventures generally include the following or some combination of the following:

- The entrepreneur's personal funds, often supplemented by funds from relatives and others,
- Borrowing from a bank or other lender (debt financing)
- Selling shares of ownership (equity) in the company

Debt financing adds interest payments to our fixed costs, but makes no claim beyond the amount of the debt no matter how great our success. Standards for debt financing are generally very difficult for startups to meet; lenders are not generally willing to share the risk with you. If you are turned down by a lender, ask them for specific reasons. If the reasons cannot be countered with this lender, the insight gained can be used to strengthen the presentation to the next.

What do we have to offer prospective investors? For most, their primary interest is in a high return on their investment, through dividends and appreciation. Other considerations might be opportunities for tax benefits, and for director and consulting income. Of generally lesser interest are non-cash rewards, such as privileged information, access to new products, and "psychic income." There is little appeal to most investors in being a long-term minority owner in a closely-held business, so some way of "cashing out," such as a provision for company buy-back, must be offered.

Some of the questions that can be used to assess our financial plan are the following:

Is startup capitalization adequate? Is it used well? Are all startup costs recognized? Are sales and sales growth expectations realistic?

Are sales projections credible? Achievable? Are expense estimates reasonable? Complete? Are margin goals realistic? Convincing? Is there a solid basis for estimates (industry norms, experience), or do they appear to be guesswork? Is the progression of income/expense estimates credible?

Are income, cash flow, and balance statements consistent? Is cash well managed? Is the cash management strategy clear? Does the total package (text, statements, assumptions, etc.) present a clear and complete picture of the financial position?

In the course of attempting to sell equity, the entrepreneur is often called upon to make a presentation to prospective investors. Be well prepared; in your rehearsal make sure that the length of the presentation is appropriate for the time allowed. Stress the benefits to the investor. End with a call to action – ask for commitments of funds.

Once the venture is funded new challenges arise.

The amount of time required for a new venture to reach profitability is a critical factor in whether or not a business survives the startup trauma. A promising new business, well on its way to viability, can still experience severe cash flow problems; sometimes these can be fatal. Even beyond the startup period, strains on cash can severely limit company growth.

Managers, particularly in survival-stage businesses, track their financial data closely. Most are very conscious of what the income statement tells them, but not enough manage the balance sheet as well. Cash is the foundation for a strong balance sheet. Proper cash management permits the owner to meet the cash needs of the business, take advantage of special buys and discounts, minimize interest expense, and ride out slow periods. A good cash position allows the owner to maintain an adequate level of inventory, replace equipment as needs arise, and to seize expansion opportunities.

Once the business rises above the survival stage the entrepreneur must decide whether this is as far as they want to go, or whether they wish to grow and expand the business. For some the current level of business generates enough income to support their lifestyle, and they don't wish to take on the risk of expansion. Others see the opportunities available for growth and wish to pursue them.

In either case the entrepreneur should closely watch the numbers that indicate how the business is doing. In addition to sales, income, and margin there are numerous financial ratios that can be calculated to allow for a finer degree of monitoring.

Strategic options in a growth situation must be identified. Can we improve market share in the current market? Should we try to sell more to current customers by widening our product line? Can we cover a broader geographic area? Are there other channels of distribution that should be considered? Is our business concept franchisable? Should we develop a branch office network? How big can we get to be? How fast can we get there?

Several options are available to the entrepreneur once the business is prosperous, the option of selling it arises. There might be an opportunity to pass the business along to the next generation, creating the need to groom a successor. In some cases the company could be sold to the employees.

A cornerstone of the successful long-term business is a commitment to ethical behavior, community involvement, and social responsibility. This commitment is tested while working for others, as we consider starting our own ventures, and on the way we treat our employees. The rewards of keeping this commitment can far exceed the monetary rewards of a successful business.

APPENDIX

Discussion of Study Questions

Chapter 1

1. The Marketing Concept
   You might look up names of existing science fiction bookstores to spur your thinking, but don't take one verbatim. In identifying customers remember that most but not all of your inventory is science fiction, and you don't want the rest to languish on the shelves.

   Is the way to reach buyers of used books any different from that for books in general? Browse the websites of similar bookstores to see how they present themselves. Note what you like about them and what you dislike. This should help give you some direction.

2. Reality Check
   How hard are you willing to work? Do you need to keep a day job for a while yet? Projections are very hard to make. We are working in the future. Are there similar local bookstores where you might browse a while and note traffic and other patterns?

3. Feasibility Study Worksheet

    The worksheet shows the minimal amount of data to provide meaningful estimates of the feasibility of the venture. This can be easily implemented in Excel. Be realistic, even conservative in estimating costs.

    There are many sales forecasting spreadsheets available online. SCORE has one example (https://www.score.org/resource/sales-forecast-12-months).

Chapter 2

1. Why is the Internet such a powerful business platform?
    a. Startup costs are minimal

    b. Business is global

    c. A small business can grow large quickly

2. Which of your business ideas lend themselves to an Internet platform?
    Examples include:

    a. Sell your handmade arts and crafts on Etsy

    b. Run an informative site that generates revenue through advertisements

    c. Provide professional services to clients around the world

    d. Generate client leads for offline businesses

e. Sell other peoples' products and earn a commission for each referral

3. What are the major tools to develop increased viewership for your website?
Search engine optimization and pay-per-click advertising

4. What are the most commonly used social media? Which are best for your application?
Facebook, Twitter, Pinterest, Instagram, Tumblr. You suggest the best for you.

5. What are some of the most important factors in online selling success?
a. The price point of the product should be somewhere between $10 and $50.

b. The product should be as light as possible.

c. Check to see if any potential competitors have a 5,000 best seller rank (BSR) or lower in their primary category.

d. Make sure there aren't any brand names within the product category or niche.

e. If possible, sell a product that isn't easily broken.

f. The more reviews a product has, the greater the competition is. Fifty or fewer reviews on first page products is a good indicator that you can break into the market.

g. The cost of manufacturing should be 25 percent or less of the actual sale price.

Chapter 3

Here are resources for researching a used book store:

"The Growing Market in Used Books," Tzu-Chen Huang and Yi-Ling Yang, accessed March 11, 2017, https://are.berkeley.edu/~sberto/UsedBooks.pdf.

"Used Books Booming Online: The BISG Study Preview," Shelf Awareness, accessed March 11, 2017, http://www.shelf-awareness.com/issue.html?issue=61#m399.

1. How would you rate the marketing plan? How is *Atlantic* differentiated from the competition? What need are they filling? Are we convinced that need exists?
   The beer would be marketed initially by competing for tap space. Its differentiation was that it was free of preservatives and made with spring water. The need, at best, was that it was a premium beer and a tastier alternative to national beers. The success of microbrewery products has demonstrated that there is a market.

2. Analyze their pricing strategy. What is their greatest competition?

It was priced with imported beers which were perceived as premium beers, and their natural competition.

3. Suggest a marketing campaign that emphasizes *Atlantic*'s strengths. To whom are we trying to appeal? What is the best way to reach them?

While the product is available only on tap it would be marketed as exclusive, available at "fine bars..." Awareness of the brand could be built with tastings at some of the larger bars in their territory. Newspaper ads for these tastings would build business and build the loyalty of the bar owners.

Chapter 4

1. How would you rate the quality of the market research used to justify the venture? What would you have done differently? What would you have done additionally? John estimated next year's sales based on the previous year but sales were increasing rather rapidly. This caused estimates to be conservative, which is probably a good thing. He could have talked to other local business people in non-competitive industries and builders who would be potential customers.

2. Given the information used in John's analysis, would you have opened the branch? Are they trying to justify opening the branch, no matter what the data showed? This decision as to whether or not to open depends entirely on your tolerance of risk. There did seem to be a bias toward opening the branch.

3. Were John's expense estimates too rough? How could they have been refined? Were the expense categories reasonable and complete? Was the market share estimate realistic?

   Certainly any estimates could be considered rough, but I feel that John did well with the quality of information available. The omitted item in the analysis was rent. The expense categories were a bit too broad. The 75% market share assumed was pretty aggressive.

Chapter 5

Mini-Case 5-1

1. Does Clay have enough information to make an offer? What else should he do? Is there any one with whom he should consult for advice?

   The poor state of the financial records make the assessment of its potential very difficult. Clay should consult his accountant, possibly for a format for Romer to present his financials.

2. How do you feel about the "intangibles?" Are you satisfied with Sam's reasons for selling the business? How do you feel about keeping him on as a salesman? The intangibles were worrisome. He had little idea of the company's profitability. Sam's reason for selling was OK, but left the feeling that he just wanted out of the business. His manner precluded hiring him as a salesman.

3. What exactly is Clay buying? Is he likely to retain existing customers? Could he not establish similar buying relationships anyway? Should he keep the technician?
He is buying inventory and a customer list. There is no guarantee that existing customers would feel obliged to do business with the new company. The technician should be interviewed with the rigor of any job applicant.

4. Does the company give Clay a "running start" in the business? Does it offer a better foundation for growth than a start-up? Is it limiting in any way?
The acquisition is essentially a new business. It would buy into a structure that looks to public sector bidding and subsequently lower margins.

5. Should Clay make a lower offer? Based on what? For how much? What should his negotiating strategy be?
He should offer an inventory purchase only, on a take-it-or-leave-it basis.

Case 5-2

1. Is John underestimating the disadvantages of independence: decreased purchasing power; loss of access to the considerably larger inventory in the Metairie warehouse, and; management depth and other synergies due to being part of a larger operation? These disadvantages were thought to be only short-term but the reality was that it took a while to overcome the decreased purchasing power associated with being what vendors considered a low-volume operation. Some lines of products were also not accessible without a minimum level of purchases.

2. Can John assume that Southland's customers will become Tammany's customers? Why would they, or why might they not? Can TSI maintain the service level they had with Southland's resources behind them? The only customers TSI lost were those with substantial operations in Metairie and New Orleans. Maintaining the service level required sometimes buying out-of-stock items from other supply houses at cost-plus, making the margin thin for such sales.

3. John is 35 years old, and knows the administrative side of the business, but not the "pieces and parts;" Buck knows the material but now, at 20 years old, has become purchasing agent as well as warehouse manager. Are they in over their heads?

A couple of strategic hires improved the situation, but TSI was overly dependent on John and Buck. The result was very long hours for both.

4. Is an arms-length transaction feasible when the buyer has so much more information than the seller? Is John's suggested price going to be acceptable?
   The financial information was available to both parties and John reported customer situations and growth expectations. Because the Southland ownership looked favorably on the transaction there was little dispute about the price.

5. Could the final price have been flexible, based on the first few years' performance of TSI? Should John have factored in the cyclical nature of the business, rather than counting on steady growth for the evaluation period?
   Perhaps an arrangement could have been made on a percentage of TSI's profits going to Southland, but it was not considered.

6. Do you agree with the evaluation process? What might you have done differently? Do you agree with the result? If you were to modify it, in which direction would you go? Should the deal happen? Is it "win-win?"
   Some consideration could have been made for projected earnings as would be the norm in sales like this, but the sale was considered "win-win."

Case 5-3

1. Was the purchase agreement with Southland really at "arm's length," or were concessions made to John that might not have been made to an outsider? Did the terms lower the effective selling price? Was Southland continuing to bear some of the risk of TSI's success? The purchase was merely that of assets where other buyers would have paid on earnings potential and a premium for a going business. Southland's only risk was on John defaulting on the inventory loan.

2. Was John overreaching his financial resources when he purchased the business? Should he have postponed the deal a year? Should he have retained the partnership in the building with his brothers? Did he leave himself any financial "cushion?" Would you have done the same?
   John was excited about the potential for the business and may have acted prematurely, but it was a measured risk with which he was comfortable.

3. How do you explain the way in which performance exceeded projections? Was one year of operating experience enough to project sales for the next three years? Did John "lowball" his sales estimates to Southland? Should John offer a supplemental payment to Southland? Could John's actions as business owner been enough different from his actions as partner to explain the difference in performance?

The growth of the area exceeded almost everyone's expectations. John proved very skilled at building and protecting market share.

4. Are two years of growth and success (mid-1998 to mid-2000) enough to justify the large additional investment made in 2000? Should it have been done more stage-wise? Is the observed growth rate sustainable? What are the consequences of it not being? Discuss in terms of company investment, and John's personal investment (building expansion).
   It had become obvious that this was a great opportunity, and the large investments were pre-emptive as other supply houses were considering locating in TSI's market area. The personal investment was a separate business, that of a commercial property manager, and was not as successful.

5. What are the implications of the competition "discovering" the Covington market? Have any barriers to entry been erected? Why could TSI drive a larger competitor out of the market? After they left, do you think they had given up on the market entirely? Certainly competition would lower margins. Larger competitors would be only as strong as the commitment they made to TSI's market. Two competitors entered the market and left soon after, but continued to keep up with how the market was building.

Chapter 6

Case Study 6-1

1. Did decisions made during the good times contribute to the difficulty of dealing with the crash? Could the assets have been managed better? Could adjustments have been made more smoothly?
   Certainly the aggressive marketing and inventory could have been lessened, but the crash was hard to predict and opportunities may have been lost had these investments not been made.

2. Should the bad times ahead have been foreseen by TSI management? Were they slow to respond? Were their actions appropriate? Effective?
   Management could have responded more quickly but that might have hurt them in the longer term, e.g., firing more people and firing them sooner.

3. Why is John so reluctant to scale the business down to a level appropriate to sales? What would the longer-term consequences be? How would the competition view such a move? What would it do to the chances for recovery as the economy improves?
   The depth that the slowdown would reach and its length were hard to predict. A weakened TSI would invite competition. Decreasing the workforce would have hampered the recovery effort.

4. What are TSI's strategic options? What information would you gather to help evaluate possible new product lines or related ventures? What new offerings would fit well with traditional plumbing supply lines? Is it better to sell more things to existing customers, or bring in new customers?

   TSI broadened the product line while letting its depth decrease. They added sprinkler systems, which sold a lot of pipe, taking business away from lawn and garden stores. Septic tanks took sales from lumberyards. Other items competed with electrical suppliers.

5. If new lines are added, is it better to re-train existing personnel or replace some with new employees experienced in the new line? If the re-train option is chosen, how long might it be before TSI can effectively market the new products?

   It is better to retrain existing personnel because they know the rest of the lines as well. Re-training was not particularly challenging, and the vendor was available for support.

6. How effectively can TSI broaden its offerings with $70,000 in cash? Would it be better to preserve the cash to ride out the difficult period? Is this any time for "adventurism," or should John concentrate on holding on to what is left of his core business?

   That amount could buy a substantial inventory of a related product. Preserving the cash could last for a short-time but is not a good longer-term strategy. One person's "adventurism" may be responsible investment to another.

7. How does John's ownership of the building, outside of TSI, affect his options? Is he caught in any conflict of objectives? Would he act differently on behalf of TSI if the building were owned by someone else? Should he try to sell the building?
Ownership of the building could provide collateral for an inventory loan. Owning the business personally would allow him to raise the rent of the corporation, which is not in the corporation's best interest. Were the business owned by someone else he might be asking for a break on the rent. A case could be made for owning the building (tax advantages?) and not (removes conflict of interest).

8. Is now the time to sell the business? Are the regional chains likely to still be interested? How fast can the business be "turned around?" What would you do?
This is not a time to sell if the business can be turned around short of bankruptcy.

Business Plan Review

1. What is the major purpose of a business plan? Is a business plan needed where the entrepreneur can finance the venture without assistance?
The purpose of a business plan is to recognize and define a business opportunity, describe how that opportunity will be seized by the management team,

and to demonstrate that the business is feasible and worth the effort.

2. What are the primary components of the business plan? Is there a standard format? An appropriate length? A specific audience for whom it is written?
   While the formats of business plans can be as varied as the businesses themselves, there are components that should appear in all plans. These include an executive summary, elements which describe the opportunity, elements which specify how the business will operate, an analysis of financial expectations, a closing summary, and any supporting documentation.

3. What are the major objectives of the marketing plan? In this section, we need to clearly delineate our niche, and our distinctive competence.

4. What are the logistical issues that should be resolved in the plan?
   How much space do we need? How much equipment? What other facilities are important? Should we buy property and equipment or lease? Which makes exit easier? How many employees do we need at startup? Is business location a significant factor? If so, what are our location criteria?

5. What is the purpose of the strategic plan?
   The strategic plan defines the company's "competitive edge," that collection of factors that sets the business

apart from its competitors and promotes its chances for success.

6. Does the form and quality of the business plan affect our chance of convincing prospective stakeholders? Aren't most investors and lenders too sophisticated to be swayed by form? How do they use the plan to evaluate us?
Certainly the form and quality indicate to the reader how invested you are in the project. Mistakes call into question your ability to put together a business which has little margin for error.

Case Study 6-2

1. Was 2007 too late for TSI to write its first business plan? Would a formal written strategic plan in 2005 have helped guide the company through the difficult period? Could it have helped soften the impact? What was the purpose of the 2010 plan?
Certainly having a plan, if it is well prepared, is better than not having a plan. The 2010 plan was essentially a recovery plan.

2. Evaluate the strategic plan. Does the assessment of external forces seem reasonable? Are internal capabilities reasonably assessed? Does the strategy selection follow logically from the assessments?
Competition was easing as rivals left the area. While getting out of the cabinet business cost some revenue,

it was not a good strategic fit. The company strategy could be said to be stressing its "core competence."

3. Are the goals expressed too modest, reasonable, or too ambitious? Are they relevant to the problems facing TSI? Are the tools necessary to their accomplishment identified?

   The goals seem responsive to the opportunities. The company is better focused and prepared for the expected growth in its core business. After a difficult period collections are under control, the inventory is fresh and new items seem to be doing well.

4. Is management in control and on target? Are they collecting the right information, and evaluating it properly, as a guide to future actions?

   Business planning has gotten more sophisticated and forms a useful basis going forward.

5. How successful has the diversification strategy been? Should it be abandoned, or simply refined? Do the reasons for dropping SKB make sense? How is SKB significantly different from the other forms of diversification?

   Diversification was successful in general with OLC a success and new inventory items a good fit. Sometimes things don't work out and SKB was just not a good strategic fit.

6. Why did two competitors move in after the crash? Why do you think they could not make it? Why were

the earlier entries small independents, while the regional chain waited until an apparent recovery was under way? What effect do you expect the 2011 entry of a competitor with "deep pockets" will have on TSI's recovery?

Competitors saw what they perceived to be a weakened TSI, but TSI had a loyal customer base that the competitors could not crack. The regional chain felt that they should wait until competition left all firms weakened. It was possible that a well-financed chain operation could "break" TSI, but they were not willing to take those kind of losses.

7. Are you confident about TSI's prospects for the remaining two years of this planning period? What would you do differently?

The prospects are good if the expected increase in construction activity comes to pass.

Chapter 8

Minicase 8-1

1. Is it possible for Carol to be giving her best to NPI in her current frame of mind? Should she continue with NPI once she begins to develop a business plan? Once she has decided that she will probably start her own firm? Once she is definite?

Carol is not giving her all to NPI. Certainly some preliminary planning can be done while employed, but it rapidly becomes a distraction.

2. Can she ethically discuss her plans with Bill Blake now? Can she begin to negotiate terms of employment with him?

   She should certainly not.begin discussing plans with a fellow NPI employee. This must wait until after she is on her own.

3. Should she approach her current customers for a written commitment to doing business with her new company to present to her banker in confidence? How would you expect her customers to react? How would her banker view such letters?

   "Poaching" NPI customers while on the NPI payroll will be viewed very negatively by the customers. The banker would also view Carol as unethical and not be favorably disposed to working with her.

Minicase 8-2

1. How applicable are norms for an entire industry to a specific small business? Are differences from norms more reflective of quality of management, operating strategies, or competitive conditions?

   Norms often are established over a large number of cases and cannot be applied strictly. Still, they can be useful, particularly when the company varies widely from the norms. Certainly management, strategy and competition are all significant factors.

2. Is rapid increase in sales volume a valid reason for a low gross margin? What is the mechanism by which

this occurs? Does an acceptable net margin validate this approach?

Rapid increases in sales are often the result of aggressive pricing which produces low margins. If we can live with the margins produced this may be a valid strategy.

3. Does a return on equity of about 10% represent an effective use of our personal resources? What are our options, and what is their likely return?

An acceptable return on equity is best established by comparing it to the return that could be achieved in other investments. If savings accounts are earning 5% then we are better off with the business. Let's say the stock market is earning 16%. We could presumably liquidate our investment and put it in the market and do better, but there is an element of risk involved, and we would lose our salary.

Growing the Business

1. What are the stages in small business growth? How can we tell which we are currently in?

The five stages are existence, survival, success, take-off, resource maturity.

2. Why is ethical behavior important to a business? Can we identify ethical attitudes of businesses with which we are familiar? Can we identify ethical challenges we have faced in our business experience?

Ethical behavior should be part of the foundation of the business. Any business has "strategic partners," such as suppliers, customers, consultants, etc. Unethical behavior with any of these can have consequences over the entire network.

3. Why is cash flow so important to the growing business? What can we do to improve the cash flow of such a business? Can cash position ever be too strong?

   Businesses can be profitable and fail for lack of the cash needed to stay in business. Should cash flow be a problem this can limit the rate of growth. If the cash position is too strong one can pay off debt, or find some other more productive way to use the excess.

4. How are the commonly used financial ratios helpful in managing a business?

   The ratios can indicate areas that may need more attention.

5. What are the common strategic options in growing a business? How do we choose between them? What are the primary limitants?

   One can improve market share in the current market, enlarge the market geographically, and broaden the market with new product lines. The business concept may be franchisable.

6. Why would a business owner not pursue a growth strategy?

Many business owners view theirs as a "lifestyle" business, that is, that they are satisfied with a good income but do not want the stress of rapid growth.

Case Study 8-1

1. Is now a good time to sell, or do prospective buyers see the same danger signs that Vinturella sees? Should he approach the firm currently considering entering the market? Can he get that firm and his current competitor into a "bidding war?"

   It would probably be a fairly good time to sell. An outside viewer would probably see the market as more promising than Vinturella did with his intimate knowledge of market factors. A sale to a company entering the market would be a strategic sale, generally a higher return transaction. A bidding war would be a positive for Vinturella.

2. Are the danger signs real or imagined? Is Vinturella just getting "gun-shy" from his earlier reverses? Would a levelling off at this sales volume adversely affect TSI's profitability?

   The dangers are real though probably not as severe as viewed by Vinturella. He does seem to be a bit more cautious than in previous years.

3. Were some of Vinturella's recent decisions those of a short-termer? Was the reversal of the diversification program short-sighted? Has the market matured to the

240

point where TSI has lost the competitive advantage of being the small, independent, locally owned firm? Vinturella has begun giving more attention to life outside TSI and this could affect some decisions. TSI's competitive advantage has weakened as more companies view the market favorably.

4. Is it smart for Vinturella to consider selling now, when his alternate sources of income are not yielding much, or should he wait until his other pursuits prove more profitable? Is it fair for him to continue to draw a substantial salary? What do you see happening to TSI's market value if he waits a year or two to offer it for sale?

   One has to evaluate offers as they arrive. Trying to time the sale requires there being a buyer when one is ready to sell, and that is not a constant. Vinturella is certainly entitled to whatever salary he cares to take. He has a great deal of capital at risk.

5. Assuming that the business might appraise for a million dollars, how much might Vinturella realize from its sale? What kind of income might that provide for life? What would the investment options be? Does he owe anything to his children?

   After bills are paid and taxes set aside he might realize $600,000. If he can find another source of income and properly invest the proceeds it could last a good while.

6. What are Vinturella's *real* reasons for considering a sale of the business? Could his sense of no longer being needed be driving it, or is it for business reasons? How might Ron and Scott react if he brought them into discussing the possibility?

   Burnout seems to be a factor I the consideration of a sale. This would also be a factor in feeling a diminished role in company success.

7. Were Vinturella to decide not to sell, are there any dangers in prolonging the current situation? Might other employees perceive it as a disinterested leader, caretaker manager, not-yet-ready successor designate? Do they care? Is it an accurate perception? How might customers and suppliers view the situation? What about competitors?

   The sense of burnout will only get worse, and with it a decrease in performance. The employees can see this and are concerned. Customers and suppliers could be a bit more careful about their commitment to TSI's being well-run and highly competitive. Competitors like what they see.

8. Can Vinturella really be the company leader on a one-day-a-week schedule? Even with his loss of interest? Are there any actions he can take, short of selling, to pass on the leadership of TSI? Can a non-owner manager be a leader? How soon can Scott take over? When should he? What are the criteria?

His leadership at one-day-a-week is best measured by what happens when he is there. Should Vinturella not choose to sell he must groom a successor. Part of this grooming is an ongoing evaluation of the successor's suitability for the role.

REFERENCES

Books

Chapter 1

1. Peter F. Drucker, *Innovation and Entrepreneurship* (New York: HarperCollins, 2009)
2. Jeffry A. Timmons and Stephen Spinelli, *New Venture Creation* (New York: McGraw-Hill/Irwin, 2008)

Websites

Chapter 1

1. "Is Entrepreneurship for You," SBA, accessed March 8, 2017, https://www.sba.gov/starting-business/how-start-business/entrepreneurship-you.
2. "Springwise," Springwise, accessed March 8, 2017, https://www.springwise.com/.
3. "11 Industries for Hot Startups," Forbes, accessed March 8, 2017, https://www.forbes.com/pictures/efgg45kmfg/11-industries-for-hot-start-ups/#56a763996c0b.

4. "How to Research Your Business Idea," Entrepreneur, accessed March 8, 2017, https://www.entrepreneur.com/article/70518.

5. "The Five Trends Marketers Can't Afford to Ignore in 2017," Little Black Book, accessed March 8, 2017, https://lbbonline.com/news/the-5-trends-marketers-cant-afford-to-ignore-in-2017.

6. "Sixteen Surprising Statistics about Small Businesses," Forbes, accessed March 8, 2017, https://www.forbes.com/sites/jasonnazar/2013/09/09/16-surprising-statistics-about-small-businesses/#28d688695ec8.

7. "Unique Selling Proposition (USP)," Entrepreneur, accessed March 8, 2017, https://www.entrepreneur.com/encyclopedia/unique-selling-proposition-usp.

8. "Sales Forecast (12 Months)," SCORE, accessed March 8, 2017, https://www.score.org/resource/sales-forecast-12-months.

Chapter 2

9. "Number of Internet Users Worldwide from 2005 to 2016," Statista, accessed March 10, 2017, https://www.statista.com/statistics/273018/number-of-internet-users-worldwide/.

10. "Why Companies Need a Website," WebDoctor, accessed March 10, 2017, http://www.dbwebdoctor.com/article_why_companies_need_a_website.asp.

11. "Seven Reasons Why You Should Start Your Own Internet Business," Lifehack, accessed March 10, 2017, http://www.lifehack.org/articles/

money/7-reasons-why-you-should-start-your-own-internet-business.html.

12. "SEO Basics: 22 Essentials You Need for Optimizing Your Site," Search Engine Watch, accessed March 10, 2017, https://searchenginewatch.com/2016/01/21/seo-basics-22-essentials-you-need-for-optimizing-your-site/.

13. "What is PPC?" WordStream, accessed March 10, 2017, http://www.wordstream.com/ppc.

14. "Social Media for Business," Business News Daily, accessed March 10, 2017, http://www.businessnewsdaily.com/7832-social-media-for-business.html.

15. "Fulfillment by Amazon Poses a Great Option for Those Looking to Break Into Ecommerce," Entrepreneur, accessed March 10, 2017, https://www.entrepreneur.com/article/252685.

16. "My Amazon FBA Journey," Passion into Paychecks, accessed March 10, 2017, https://www.passionintopaychecks.com/my-amazon-fba-journey/.

17. "What the Most Successful FBA Sellers Do Differently," TeikaMetrics, accessed March 10, 2017, http://blog.teikametrics.com/2015/07/what-the-most-successful-fba-sellers-do-differently-webinar-recap.html.

18. "Our Unbiased Comparison of Amazon and Ebay," eBridge Connections, accessed March 10, 2017, http://www.ebridgeconnections.com/Media/Blog/

June-2015/OUR-UNBIASED-COMPARISON-OF-
AMAZON-AND-EBAY.aspx.

Chapter 3

19. "Why golf is in decline in America," Economist, accessed March 11, 2017, http://www.economist. com/blogs/economist-explains/2015/04/economist-explains-1.
20. "Emerging Trends in the Remodeling Market," Joint Center for Housing Studies of Harvard University, accessed March 11, 2017, http://www. jchs.harvard.edu/sites/jchs.harvard.edu/files/ jchs_improving_americas_housing_2015_final.pdf
21. "Census.Gov," United States Census Bureau, accessed March 11, 2017, http://www.census.gov.

Chapter 4

22. "Start-Up Expenses," SCORE. Accessed March 12, 2017, https://www.score.org/resource/start-expenses.

Chapter 5

23. "The Little Black Book of Billionaire Secrets," Forbes, accessed March 15, 2017, https://www.forbes.com/sites/ kenrapoza/2013/02/18/one-in-five-americans-work-from-home-numbers-seen-rising-over-60/#905eb7e25c1d.
24. "Best Products to Sell from Home," The Work at Home Woman, accessed March 16, 2017, https://www. theworkathomewoman.com/best-products-sell-home/

25. "Home Based Business Statistics In America," Business for Home, accessed March 16, 2017, https://www.businessforhome.org/2012/07/home-based-business-in-america/

26. "The Advantages and Disadvantages of Working from Home," Bayt, accessed March 16, 2017, https://www.bayt.com/en/career-article-1601/

27. "Quick Franchise Facts Franchising Industry Statistics," AZ Franchises, accessed March 16, 2017, http://www.azfranchises.com/quick-franchise-facts/.

Chapter 7

28. "Crowdfunding," Investopedia, accessed March 20, 2017, http://www.investopedia.com/terms/c/crowdfunding.asp

29. "SEC Democratizes Equity Crowdfunding With JOBS Act Title IV," Forbes, accessed March 20, 2017, https://www.forbes.com/sites/chancebarnett/2015/03/26/infographic-sec-democratizes-equity-crowdfunding-with-jobs-act-title-iv/#7e71056c73eb

30. "26 Best Crowdfunding Sites by Niche," Wrike, accessed March 20, 2017, https://www.wrike.com/blog/26-top-crowdfunding-sites-by-niche/

31. "Accredited Investors," U.S. Securities and Exchange Commission, accessed March 20, 2017, https://www.sec.gov/fast-answers/answers-accredhtm.html

INDEX

A

accountable 26

accounts receivable 99, 105, 110, 130, 152, 170, 173, 182, 213

advertising 35, 42, 43, 55, 74, 82, 83, 90, 129, 134, 151, 156, 200, 204, 212, 221

Amazon 46, 47, 48, 49, 247, 248

appreciation 160, 216

assertive 26

assets 84, 92, 95, 97, 99, 100, 102, 104, 105, 109, 110, 113, 124, 132, 152, 153, 154, 162, 166, 173, 174, 176, 192, 207, 208, 213, 214, 228, 230

assumptions 36, 41, 58, 92, 93, 95, 103, 136, 155, 162, 207, 216

B

balance sheet 99, 105, 113, 151, 152, 153, 169, 170, 171, 187, 208, 213, 214, 217

breakeven 71, 72, 74, 75, 76, 77, 93, 101, 108, 203, 207

business ix, x, xii, xiii, 1, 2, 3, 4, 5, 6, 7, 8, 9, 10, 11, 12, 13, 14, 15, 17, 19, 20, 21, 22, 23, 24, 25, 26, 27, 28, 29, 30, 31, 32, 38, 39, 40, 41, 43, 44, 45, 46, 47, 48, 49, 50, 52, 53, 54, 55, 56, 58, 59, 60, 61, 62, 63, 64, 65, 66, 69, 72, 76, 77, 78, 79, 80, 81, 82, 83, 84, 88, 89, 91, 92, 93, 94, 95, 96, 97, 98, 99, 101, 105, 106, 107, 108, 109, 112, 114, 115, 116, 117, 118, 119, 120, 121, 122, 123, 124, 125, 126, 130, 131, 132, 133, 135, 136, 137, 138, 139, 140, 141, 142, 143, 144, 145, 146, 148, 150, 151, 152, 153, 154, 155, 156, 157, 158, 160, 161, 162, 163, 164, 165, 166, 167, 168, 169, 170, 172, 174, 175, 176, 177, 178, 179, 180, 181, 182, 183, 184,

V

W